THE SAVE BRITAIN'S HERITAGE ACTION GUIDE

THE SAVE BRITAIN'S HERITAGE ACTION GUIDE

**MARCUS BINNEY &
MARIANNE WATSON-SMYTH**

COLLINS & BROWN

ILLUSTRATION ACKNOWLEDGEMENTS

Arundell House 101; Ian Beesley 130; Marcus Binney 66, 145; *Country Life* 108; Malcolm Crowthers 16; Ken Done 54; English Heritage 36; Mark Fiennes frontispiece, 58, 94; Frith Collection 141; Michael Hopkins 103; The Landmark Trust 70; Randolph Langenbach 134; Alan McPherson 12; Trevor Mitchell 92; Keith Parkinson 34, 85, 119, 132; Giles Quarme 125; RCHME 34, 52, 67, 78, 83, 90; RCHMW 46; *Rugby Advertiser* 78; SAVE 34, 40, 49; Joseph Sharples 14; Morley von Sternberg 122; Huw Thomas 75; Thoresby Estate 43; *The Times* 78, 97; Marianne Watson-Smyth 96; Colin Westwood 13

FRONTISPIECE: *Cresswell Mill, Derbyshire*

First published in Great Britain in 1991
by Collins & Brown Limited
Mercury House
195 Knightsbridge
London SW7 1RE

Copyright © Collins & Brown 1991

Text copyright © SAVE 1991

The right of SAVE to be identified as the author of this work has been asserted by it in accordance with the Copyright, Designs and Patents Act 1988.

All rights reserved. No part of this publication may be reproduced, stored in a retrieval system, or transmitted in any form or by any means electronic, mechanical, photocopying, recording or otherwise, without the prior written permission of the copyright owner.

A CIP catalogue record for this book is available from the British Library

ISBN 1 85585 056 7

Conceived, edited and designed by Collins & Brown Limited

Editorial Director: Gabrielle Townsend

Editors: Elizabeth Drury
Sarah Bloxham

Designers: Ruth Hope
Claire Graham

Filmset by J&L Composition Ltd, Filey, North Yorkshire
Printed and bound in Great Britain by The Bath Press, Avon

CONTENTS

Why Save?	7
The Origins of SAVE	10
What You Can Do	18
SAVE in Action	31

    Causes and Campaigns 32 Country Houses 33 Country House Parks 61 Gardens 65 Garden Buildings, Follies and Temples 69 Barns and Other Farm Buildings 73 Churches 77 Town Buildings 99 Interiors 106 Preserving Facades 110 Shopfronts 113 Street Furniture 116 Markets 118 Hospitals and Asylums 124 Industrial Buildings 128 Railway Stations and Structures 137 Pubs and Hotels 140 Theatres, Cinemas and Public Buildings 143 Public Parks 147

Future Agenda	148
Appendices	154

    What Listing Means 154
    SAVE Publications 154
    List of Organizations 157

Index	159

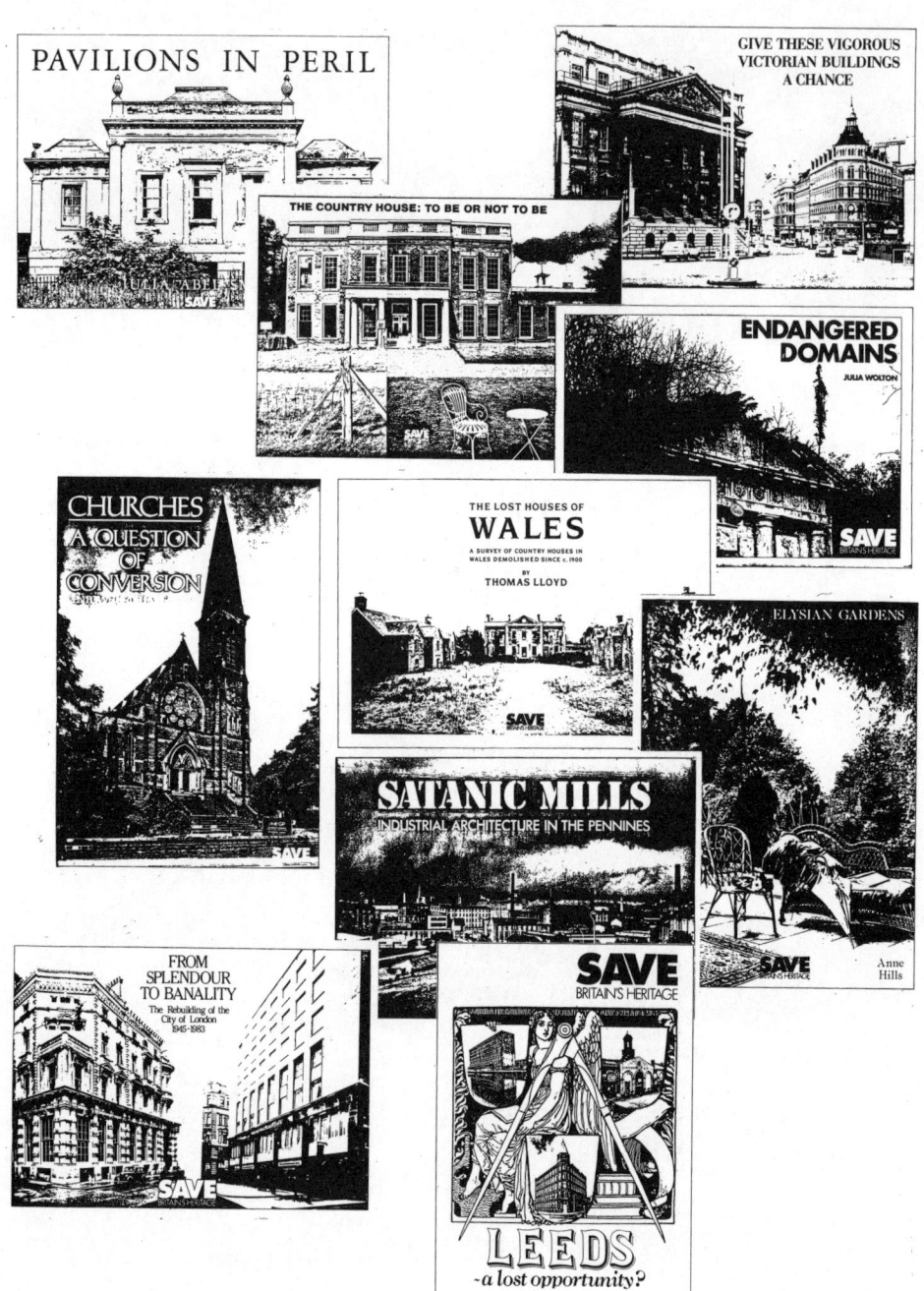

Montage of SAVE reports

WHY SAVE?

IT HAS BECOME one of the clichés of political debate that a concern for conservation is a new—and therefore probably transient—phenomenon and in addition that it is the hobby of an élite determined to fight against the inevitable overriding dictates of modern economic growth.

Neither cliché is true. As long as man has lain stone on stone, people have argued the need to show a respect for the work of their forebears. This respect has always had to be defended—in architecture, as in painting, sculpture and archaeology. And the fact that today this respect has to be defended even more stridently than before is more a comment on the destructiveness of modern development than the result of any new-fangled obsession with antiquity.

Certainly it was once hoped, particularly after the devastation of the last war, that modern architecture might with the aid of science and technology provide mankind with a wholly satisfying new environment—and do so in a matter of a few decades. Few people still believe that today. Yet the past twenty-five years have seen in the pursuit of that ideal the centres of Britain's towns and cities ripped apart, homes lost, businesses destroyed and the civilizing influence of visual continuity in our surroundings dissipated. No sensitive person can today walk through the redeveloped areas of British towns and feel a sense of pride in the architectural and social achievement they represent.

SAVE believes that modern architecture and planning is producing an environment that is not only a visual disgrace—a judgment with which future generations may conceivably disagree—but is becoming an economic and ecological nonsense as well. It is our contention that architectural conservation should be accorded the same consideration which is already being shown to the conservation of other resources, both natural and man-made, and for the same reasons.

Nowadays we literally cannot afford to neglect the investment, the hard financial investment, stored in our built environment. Buildings—and not just historic ones—represent energy, labour and materials, which either cannot be replaced or can only be replaced at enormous cost. The fight to save particular buildings or groups of buildings is not the fancy of some impractical antiquarian. It is part of a battle for the sane use of all our resources.

Any architect knows that, as a rule, old buildings are more soundly built than new ones. Benefiting from the cheaper labour and materials of the past, they are more solid, more soundproof, and better retainers of heat. Unlike a factory which depends for its efficiency on changing technology, the investment of labour, materials and energy represented in a building continues to yield a return even centuries after its construction. When it is demolished it is lost for good and can only be duplicated at considerable expense. Most historic buildings are remarkably adaptable. Contrary to one of the fantasies of modern architecture, brick and masonry buildings are far more flexible than concrete, steel-framed ones.

In the past, one of the cornerstones of the economic argument for conservation was its value to tourism. This argument was slighted by those who felt that the tourist was more concerned with a modern hotel than an ancient mansion, but the case can no longer be treated so flippantly. Tourism is now the largest single item in world trade and in cities such as London it towers over all other features of the urban economy. The desire to travel—especially among the young and the well-educated—depends not only on the existence of a few Great Sights, but also on scenic variety, a sense that a particular place is different and, above all, old. Tourists see in British domestic architecture qualities which those whose job it is to protect them often ignore. No-one can have shown Americans round cities such as London, Brighton or Bristol and not been subjected to gasps of horror when they see the depredation wrought on them by ill-sited high buildings and demolished streets.

Previously, some of the most ardent opponents of architectural conservation have themselves been architects. The reason, quite simply, is that architects find work where the market for their skill is most lucrative, and in Britain that tends to be on sites where intensive development has taken place for generations, particularly the commercial centres and inner suburbs of big cities. New buildings here usually entail the demolition of old ones, and the 'better' sites, the old ones, are often very fine ones. Conservation, however, does not mean no work for architects. The presence of the old can be a beneficial discipline, if not an inspiration, to the new. Indeed, many of our most cherished buildings derive their quality from responding to their built surroundings. The practising architect may design better buildings after working with the old ones.

Only part of the case for answering positively to the question Why save? has been given. Much more could be said. We know that the stability signified by unchanging buildings is psychologically valuable, particularly in a violent and rapidly changing world. The visible link with

WHY SAVE?

the past that old buildings give is important both as a fascinating insight into history and as an expression of the relative permanence of civilized society. Demolition has often involved appalling social disruption where not only the fabric of the building but also families, businesses and communities have been broken up. The pain and deprivation caused by the loss of the personal heritage of home, cherished street or familiar surroundings has been cruelly underestimated.

Conservation, to architect and public alike, is not a fad, a fetter or a curse: it is a necessity which should also be seen as a stimulating challenge.

Extract from the first SAVE report, the *Architects' Journal*, December 1975

THE ORIGINS OF SAVE

THE IDEA OF a new organization championing endangered historic buildings grew out of 'The Destruction of the Country House', the first major exhibition Roy Strong held at the Victoria and Albert Museum in 1974 following his appointment as Director. This was organized by two of the founders of SAVE, Marcus Binney and John Harris.

For the exhibition, a list was compiled of over 1,200 houses demolished between 1875 and 1974. No less than 625 had been lost since 1945. These losses reached a peak in 1955 when seventy-five such houses were demolished—one every five days.

The focal point of the exhibition was a giant Hall of Destruction modelled on Giulio Romano's famous painted room at the Palazzo del Tè in Mantua. The main difference here was that each stone of the tumbling columns was mounted with a photograph of a major country house destroyed in the last hundred years. The effect was dramatic and startling.

This list of destruction was sent to every newspaper in the country and the press cuttings rolled in. Virtually every paper responded, from the main provincial dailies and evening papers down to the smallest local weekly, each with a feature article on a lost house in their area. A massive public interest in—and concern for—our vanishing heritage was evident, as was the need to do something about it.

SAVE Britain's Heritage was founded in the following March, 1975. Though officially designated European Architectural Heritage Year, listed buildings, we calculated, were disappearing at the rate of one a day. If this pace kept up, 10,000 buildings classed as 'historic' would disappear over the next twenty-five years.

Faced with this potential loss, it was hardly surprising that the UK Heritage Year poster proclaimed the aim of 'calling the attention of the European people to the steady erosion of their common architectural heritage'. However, Heritage Year, we felt, would simply provide another occasion, of which there were already far too many, for Britain's architects,

THE ORIGINS OF SAVE

town planners and local authorities to pat each other on the back and give themselves awards. While the country's heritage vanished at an ever-faster rate, our town centres would sprout cosmeticized precincts and flower boxes and hold congratulatory receptions. Hardly a warning note would be sounded about the 'erosion' of anything, except perhaps the ratepayer's purse.

The first SAVE report was a manifesto, published in the *Architects' Journal* in December 1975. The report catalogued and illustrated the losses, the threats and the success stories, and also included a list of recommendations. One of these was for the creation of a new statutory historic buildings committee. This was established by Act of Parliament as the Historic Buildings and Monuments Commission for England—known as English Heritage—but not until nine years later.

Almost all the members of SAVE's initial committee were under thirty and the first starry-eyed plans of raising £15,000 in the City to set up a well-equipped office and a secretary for one year came to nothing. So a new tactic was adopted and each put in £10, raising a further £200 to £300 from friends. A rent-free office in a decayed basement in Bedford Square was found and a voluntary secretary recruited. SAVE then wrote to local newspapers all over the country appealing to amateur photographers to take photographs of endangered buildings.

It is interesting to see where the original team has gone. Simon Jenkins is Editor of *The Times*, Colin Amery Architectural Critic for the *Financial Times*. Peter Burman has become Director of the Institute of Advanced Architectural Studies in York and Margaret Richardson is Assistant Curator at the Sir John Soane Museum. David Pearce has been Secretary of the Society for the Protection of Ancient Buildings and Timothy Cantell Assistant Secretary of the Royal Society of Arts. Gillian Darley has written and presented a series of books and television programmes. Matthew Saunders, SAVE's second Secretary, now runs the Ancient Monuments Society and the Friends of Friendless Churches, and Sophie Andreae, his successor, is Head of the London Division of English Heritage.

Looking back over the years, the initial aim of creating awareness has been substantially achieved. The days when fine buildings could be demolished without anyone knowing or objecting are largely over.

Much of SAVE's work takes the form of responses to Mayday calls from local people concerned about the imminent loss of a local landmark. Recently, SAVE has been to the rescue of a small but delightful Methodist chapel in a Lincolnshire village, to stop it being dismantled and shipped to the USA; the Pavilion Theatre at Ryde on the Isle of Wight, which the local council had agreed to demolish; and a popular Hampstead pub, Jack Straw's Castle, which, though an important work by the architect Raymond Erith, the brewers wished to alter radically.

As we write, battles include a handsome Victorian set of stables in Enfield, Hertfordshire—a home for retired ponies which the local council

SAVE ACTION GUIDE

Methodist Chapel, Sproxton, Lincolnshire. This was to have been sold and shipped to America but fierce opposition has kept the chapel in its place

wants to close; Brocklesby railway station—a delightful example of a country station built for the local landlord but empty and decaying; the grade II* listed Belgrave Chapel in Darwen, Lancashire, with its Gothic pinnacles dominating the town but under threat of demolition; and the beautiful but overgrown park and gardens of Uffington in Lincolnshire, in danger of being smothered by executive homes, a golf club and a hotel.

What occupies SAVE's attention and energies most is the extraordinary number of listed buildings that are simply left empty and decaying. A listed building is one that has been officially recognized as having the right to special protection (see also What Listing Means, Appendix I, page 154). SAVE has published a whole series of reports on country houses at risk, entitled *Tomorrow's Ruins*, *Silent Mansions* and *Endangered Domains*, illustrating fine houses under threat. The rewarding part is that over two thirds usually find new owners or new uses within two years.

In 1989 SAVE's *Empty Quarters* included every kind of listed building from cottages to a cathedral (the Roman Catholic Cathedral in Middlesborough). The response was enormous and the report was covered by the national newspapers, property writers and glossy magazines. A vast number of people dream of rescuing and restoring a historic building, and a remarkable percentage actually do it. The challenge is to match the supply with the demand.

The problem with these abandoned buildings is rarely simply a matter of finance. Most of them are in legal trouble. They belong to owners who

THE ORIGINS OF SAVE

believe they have passed the point of no return or who simply do not want anyone else living on their land. A quite surprising number belong to people who simply cannot be bothered.

In such cases a sudden rush of interest can persuade an owner to sell. If he rebuffs all approaches and continues to let a listed house decay, then the local planning authority has powers to serve a Repairs Notice. This requires that the owner carry out certain specified repairs. In the last resort the council has powers to send in workmen to carry out emergency repairs with or without the owner's agreement, preventing further decay and making the building wind- and water-tight. As the council is entitled to send the bill to the owner, many decide at this stage to put the building up for sale and usually a buyer quickly comes forward.

Many of our most difficult cases are those where buildings belong not to private owners but to institutions or government organizations. All too often when they cease to use a building, they simply lock the door and walk away. What was a potentially valuable, or at least useful, asset in bricks and mortar rapidly becomes a liability.

The scenario repeats itself again and again: the rainwater gutters are choked with leaves and self-seeded grass; damp seeps through the roof and, as the building is often boarded up and not properly ventilated, perfect conditions soon exist for an outbreak of dry rot.

Jack Straw's Castle, Hampstead. An unusual building of the 1960s, radical alterations to which would have destroyed its character

13

SAVE ACTION GUIDE

Belgrave Chapel, a major landmark of Darwen, Lancashire. An application for demolition is being considered by the Department of the Environment

A building that is obviously empty immediately attracts the attention of vandals. They may not be deliberately malicious, just children looking for a little adventure, but soon windows are smashed and the doors forced open. Then the building becomes prey to something much more serious: arson—a vicious crime that all too many supposedly responsible organizations seem happy to let flourish.

Take the example of Holy Trinity, Burnley. This was included in SAVE's report, *Empty Quarters*. It produced several serious expressions of interest. Planning permission was granted for converting the church into a nursing home—an appropriate community use for a redundant church.

But Holy Trinity was not only left empty, it was left open, despite repeated pleas and warnings. Sure enough, the entire church was gutted by fire and the next day the Church authorities responded by saying they would now seek to demolish the church. The danger is, once people acquire an appetite for burning buildings down, sooner or later they will set fire to one with someone inside.

Churches are only one example of a whole range of buildings becoming redundant, which includes railway stations, textile mills, hospitals and great naval dockyards. The problem in virtually every case is that the department within the organization that uses the building is quite separate from the one that disposes of it. Usually, there is no communication between the two until the last minute, and then a long-winded procedure

THE ORIGINS OF SAVE

begins in which the empty listed building must be offered to every other part of the organization (most of which self-evidently will not want it); and while the papers sit in in-trays the repair bill escalates into hundreds of thousands of pounds.

Lancashire Evening Telegraph, *10 August 1990*

SAVE's challenge is to help find suitable new uses for the buildings. There is of course nothing new in finding new uses: Malmesbury Abbey after the Reformation became Britain's first clothing factory.

Osbert Lancaster did some memorable cartoons for the V & A's 'Country House' exhibition in which he caricatured the unsuitable new uses to which the great houses of fiction might have been put had they existed in real life. Peacock's Crotchet Castle was surrounded by gravel workings; Disraeli's Bentham was decaying behind Ministry of Defence barbed wire; and the lawns of Jane Austen's Mansfield Park were engulfed by the classrooms of a girls' school.

The encouraging surprise on visiting most empty country houses is to find that their setting is largely unspoilt. The glorious views to and from the building remain, and their grounds, though overgrown, can quickly be restored. The key to a good use is that it brings people to the building who value it for its beauty and appreciate and enjoy its surroundings—not simply people who regard it as an opportunity to acquire a large amount of cheap floor space.

SAVE ACTION GUIDE

Time and again we have seen large country houses taken over for institutional use, whether as corporate headquarters or hospitals. Initially everyone welcomes the idea, but very quickly the organization outgrows the house and goes to the local authority demanding permission to build in the grounds. 'If we can't expand', they say, 'we'll have to leave the area and dozens of jobs will be lost.' But in due course there is a change of management or a major series of cuts and the building is suddenly vacated. Anyone buying the house is faced with the problem of demolishing all the extensions if it is ever to be restored to its former glory. In fact, what inevitably happens is that someone buys the house for the floor space of the extensions, seeing the opportunity for yet further building in the grounds, where planning permission would never normally be given.

In cities and towns, equally, the preservation of old buildings also offers significant public benefits. In the last four decades, Modernist architects, with their emphasis on function, have despised what they call 'facadism' with the implication that a facade is a sham. But the fact is that most traditional streets are indeed largely a collection of facades. Taken together, they form something much more important: street architecture, which may just as well be a delightful jumble as the carefully planned composition of a Georgian terrace.

Lively, attractive streets depend on a mixture of uses at ground-floor level. This variety creates a very different kind of street to the large corporate headquarters running the length of a block with a single front door in the centre.

The Mappin and Webb triangle in the heart of the City of London

THE ORIGINS OF SAVE

Working with the architect Terry Farrell, we set out to show how the delightful triangular blocks of Victorian chambers along Queen Victoria Street in the City—Mappin and Webb is the best known—could be refurbished and brought back to life.

The appeal of the area lies in the range of shops, restaurants, sandwich bars and wine bars, and the very large and well-patronized pub, The Green Man. They open on to not only the main thoroughfares but also narrow alleys like Bucklersbury, which are so characteristic of the City and are rapidly being transformed out of recognition.

The redevelopment proposals put forward for the site at first envisaged that all the shopping should go underground. City shopkeepers thought this would be disastrous as the last thing that people cooped up in offices all day want to do is to plunge underground when at last they have a chance to get out in the fresh air.

The present proposals, which SAVE has long opposed, no longer include a massive tower block, but involve building over ancient alleys and replacing a delightful mixture of frontages with a single, monolithic block, much more bulky than the buildings now on the site.

Many of the letters we receive come from people living in country towns and villages concerned about proposals that would smother green fields with development, destroy attractive open spaces within the built-up area or ruin important views. Such people are often branded as 'NIMBYs' (Not In My Back Yard), but there is nothing wrong with seeking to safeguard the beauty of the place you live in.

The purpose of this book is not only to show how threats to our heritage can be successfully resisted but also to suggest ways of putting forward constructive alternatives. Rarely, if ever, is it actually a choice between progress and preservation, people and buildings, living communities and museum towns. Old buildings and streets, well cared for and adapted to today's needs, vastly enhance the quality of life. Let us be enriched and stimulated by the products of all ages, not just our own.

WHAT YOU CAN DO

WHY IS IT that conservation areas in our cities, towns and villages are such popular places in which to live, work and shop? Why is it so pleasant to walk down a particular street, drive through a country village with its church, cottages and farms, or visit a country house and gardens? Britain's historic buildings—of all types—have a vitally important role to play in our daily lives.

Without even realizing it, we are constantly passing and using historic buildings and areas, visiting the local library or town hall, high street shops, the cinema or pub, the public park or the hospital.

Some will be recognized as being of architectural and historic value, but there are others of more modest appearance which would nevertheless be sorely missed if they disappeared. On the whole, these are the buildings most vulnerable to demolition.

However, we are still faced with proposals for unsuitable new developments threatening the setting of more outstanding buildings; and hundreds of listed buildings and churches stand empty and neglected, and at risk.

Many people think it is hard to assess whether a building is worth preserving and ask what the criteria are for trying to save it. At SAVE we ask ourselves three simple questions:

1. **How important, architecturally or historically, is the building?**

If it is listed, then it has been officially recognized by a qualified historic building inspector as being of special interest; it has statutory protection and, in the words of the government circular, 'warrants every effort being made to preserve it'. (See also What Listing Means, Appendix I, page 154.) Buildings are not listed lightly: they have to come up to strict standards to qualify.

If it is not listed, should it be? There are still many buildings that are not listed simply because they have not yet been properly surveyed, or have somehow slipped through the net.

WHAT YOU CAN DO

Even though it may not qualify for listing, the building may have interesting features—architectural details, original doors or internal fittings. It may be that the weathered materials from which it is built are particularly attractive and there is something about the building that is pleasing to the eye—soft red brick or golden stone, patterned brickwork or decorative ironwork.

2. Is the building within a conservation area?

Many buildings make a significant contribution to the local scene and may be an important part of the townscape. A church with its spire or tower will be a noticeable landmark. A row of Victorian town houses will be an attractive element of the street. The corner shop still with its original shopfront may be a rare survivor in a redeveloped area. Once demolished, these buildings will be missed.

Conservation areas are areas of special interest and historic character. They are designated by local authorities which must then pay special attention to any applications to demolish or build anew within the area's boundaries.

Even if a building is not listed, special consent must be sought to demolish it; so conservation area designation (see page 26) is a useful form of protection for unlisted buildings.

3. If the building is no longer needed for its original purpose, could it be put to a new use?

SAVE believes, and has proved time and time again, that all types of historic buildings can have a new lease of life through conversion, offering potential and exciting challenges for developers and architects. Some of the most imaginative and interesting places to work and visit are converted historic buildings. They have proved enormously successful in both commercial and aesthetic terms.

Even if the building is in poor repair, modern building techniques are able to solve many structural problems that were deemed insoluble some years ago.

Building conservation is environmentally friendly; it is a way of using existing resources for an end-product that is unique and irreplaceable.

One more question you might ask yourself is: Is it Worth the Fight? If you feel that it will be too much of an uphill struggle to save a building, take heart from others' achievements.

Fifteen years ago, many of the cases SAVE was involved with caused ridicule amongst our critics.

But the recognition since of the tremendous value of historic buildings of all types, the successful conversion of buildings for new uses and a public determination that history will not repeat itself in terms of the demolition and desecration that was then taking place, have inspired us—and many local amenity societies, preservation trusts, action groups and individuals—to carry on campaigning.

SAVE ACTION GUIDE

Forming an action group

You may wonder: Who am I to set myself up? What special knowledge do I have? Whom do I represent? Do not delay because of these doubts. Remember, one of the fundamental freedoms is the right of free association. You and your neighbours, colleagues and soulmates are free to meet and set up a voluntary organization with almost any aim in mind. Make use of this freedom.

These are your two immediate tasks:

1. To formulate your message

Make your case crisply and succinctly, comprehensively but not exhaustively. Say why the building is worth preserving, describing briefly its architecture, history and contribution to the local scene.

Support this if you can by suitable quotes from local people, local literature or the national conservation bodies.

2. To get the message across

Make contact with people sympathetic to your cause. Explain the problem and enlist their support.

Get in touch with SAVE and other relevant bodies listed on page 158.

A telephone call alerting them briefly to the problem followed up by a letter is usually the most effective approach. Give details of the building, its address, owner, condition and use.

Send photographs if available; if not, take some and forward them as soon as possible.

SAVE and other local and national bodies can support you by making direct contact with the local planning office and writing letters of support to the local press and planners.

Identify the local politicians who are likely to be the most sympathetic.

Get ready to contact the press about publicity for your campaign (see Use of the Media, page 22).

The campaign

Two questions you will constantly be asked are: What can be done with the old wreck? and What will it cost and won't it be a waste of taxpayers' money?

It is not essential to be able to answer these questions immediately. In your initial blast, concentrate on the building's importance and interest, and the immediacy of the threat.

The immediate counterattack is simple: Has the building been offered for sale on the open market?

Michael Heseltine, when Secretary of State for the Environment, introduced a simple test, which is now permanently enshrined in the planning circulars: permission will not normally be granted for the demolition of a listed building unless it has been offered for sale on the open market, preferably freehold.

WHAT YOU CAN DO

In SAVE's experience, most listed buildings under imminent threat have not been offered for sale. And if they have been on the market the terms have often been unreasonable, with little attempt made to advertise them.

Getting professional advice
Very often the developers will produce figures showing that the building would be impossibly expensive to restore. In addition, there may be statements from engineers or surveyors suggesting that the building is physically unsound.

These must be challenged or rebutted. Today there are very few old buildings so structurally unsound that they cannot be saved. Many so-called 'expert reports' simply provide the answers sought by those who commissioned them.

You must therefore find an architect, engineer or surveyor who has experience of old buildings and can provide an alternative, independent view. In many cases this will be most heartening.

In almost all cases, the national societies can suggest local professionals who will be willing to help, sometimes on a voluntary basis.

Raising a fighting fund
Try to establish a basic float by persuading friends and well-wishers to contribute a few pounds: £20, £30 or £50 should be sufficient. SAVE itself was started on little more than £300, with initial committee members each putting in £10.

Try to obtain free services wherever possible. The cost of photocopying can mount up if you have to go to a local shop and pay several pence a sheet, whereas there are very likely to be local supporters who have photocopiers and are willing to run off a hundred copies at no charge.

Producing literature
This does not need to be smart or expensive. Make it as attention-grabbing as possible. Good, snappy headlines and bold lettering help. Thick felt-tip pens can be used to good effect.

Obtain the best photographs you can. Most photocopiers can produce reasonably good images from photographs, including colour snaps. Perhaps the local paper will take photographs for a story and make copies available to you afterwards.

Petitions
The more public support you can demonstrate, the stronger your case will be. Where there is a real emergency, the best tactic is to go straight out on to the street and recruit signatures. This raises public awareness and the press is always interested in hard statistics; so if you can say several hundred people signed the petition in an afternoon or over the course of a few days it will undoubtedly earn you publicity.

Of course there will always be some who say, 'People will sign anything', and deride your efforts. Point out that this is an extremely undemocratic and élitist attitude, particularly if it comes from public figures.

Another method is to send out a letter or leaflet with a petition form to several hundred people, inviting them to recruit signatures. They can then absorb the literature in their own time and make up their own minds. If they then go out and collect signatures no-one can say that the petition has been organized by a small group who have twisted arms in the street.

The petition can have a simple heading, such as 'Save the Congleton Arms!', or if you prefer it can be addressed to, say, the chairman of the local planning committee or the leader of the council and be slightly fuller in wording. You must none the less be sure to avoid any contentious or complicated wording, which might deter people, and choose a clear simple message, such as 'The Congleton Arms is a building of historic interest and deserves to be preserved as part of the town's heritage.'

If you are circulating a petition, be sure to put the address to which it should be returned.

Use of the media

SAVE was founded in the belief that endangered historic buildings are news. Only by drawing the attention of the public to these threats would the buildings we cared about ever be saved. Mobilizing public opinion has been our watchword from the start.

Of course, there is another view. This was put by an MP of long experience to the House of Commons Environment Committee: 'If you want to save these buildings, you will only save them by stealth.'

The root of our belief is that people do care about the places where they live, work and shop, that they are concerned about the devastation meted out to historic towns since the Second World War. Simon Jenkins made the point forcefully: 'Go to any public meeting on an environmental issue and you will find it far better attended, with feelings running far higher, than any political meeting held in the same place.'

Articles in the local press are extremely effective. Most local papers are sympathetic to heritage stories and will give space to them, particularly if there is an imminent threat. But even if the paper has been hostile do not be discouraged. Be sure to put your case as clearly and strongly as possible. It is important that you appear positive and optimistic.

Equally, do not be discouraged by hostile letters to the editor or even hostile editorials. Controversy adds to the debate and increases coverage. The more publicity you get, the more people will be likely to support you.

Compiling and using a press list Many organizations have press lists, which they keep as closely guarded secrets. The truth is that reporters are constantly swapping jobs and assignments and that your contacts may be away when you most need them. So, while it is always worth seeking out the names of journalists who have a special interest in your subject, and if appropriate sending the releases to them at home as well as to their office, always be sure to send your releases to the newsdesk and perhaps to one or two others on the paper too if it is appropriate.

WHAT YOU CAN DO

Find out which reporters on the local newspaper and radio are most likely to be interested. You can do this simply by thumbing through back copies of the newspaper and seeing who writes environmental articles. Likewise, ring up the radio station and find out who reports on these subjects.

Radio and television   Local radio stations are usually hungry for news and will be keen to interview anybody with a strong point of view. This is a key opportunity to get your case across. Stress the appeal of the building and make as much as you can of its history and contribution to the street.

Good television news coverage is of course a fantastic bonus, though it may be difficult to get for a modest but charming building. Ring the local television newsroom. There, they are likely to listen sympathetically and you may be lucky and catch them on a quiet day. But do not be downhearted if your story is not taken up, or indeed ousted at the last moment because a major story comes up: your campaign will not suffer in the long run.

Press releases   It was Simon Jenkins who set out the basic *modus operandi* for SAVE's initial work—the press release.

Press releases must be pithy, and full of substance and strong, clear comment. Be positive about what you are trying to achieve; try to avoid words such as 'saddened', 'ruinous', 'hopeless'. The release must contain all the relevant information—and preferably local contacts as well—that a journalist will need to write the story. The press will be looking for a strong statement of your own point of view, but you must not present a wholly one-sided picture. Be sure to say why owners wish to demolish a building, however strongly you may disagree with their view. A reporter has to present both sides of the picture and the developer may not be willing to speak to the press.

Reporters like facts, dates, statistics and, above all, the 'juicy quote'. Every press release should include a quotable, provocative statement from an officer or committee member of the organization involved.

Press releases should be eye-catching and on boldly headed paper. They do not need to be too smart; in fact, it is better if they do look rapidly produced, in response to an immediate threat. If they look too much like actual print, a reporter may have the feeling that the story has already been printed, and it will be less likely to catch his or her eye. It may, for instance, be better to leave type unjustified in the right margin. Leave the PR firms to produce the glossy releases and charge their clients accordingly, and let yours look like the raw news that it is.

The vital part is that the press comes to rely on your releases, knowing first that they contain newsworthy stories, and second that the facts can be depended upon. Reporters are constantly under pressure and if they feel that stories must be double-checked on every point they will not use them.

The key point in writing a press release is to encapsulate the message in the first sentence. Do not fall into the trap of trying to write an introductory paragraph setting the situation in context; you are not writing an essay. The main aim is to catch the interest of the reader in the first few phrases.

You do not need to send your releases to everyone who might be interested if this is likely to delay getting them into the post; that can always be done the next morning. People will still receive them at the same time the story appears in the newspaper. However, it is important to keep your fellow campaigners in other groups informed of what you are doing as the likelihood is that they will read your releases and help circulate them further.

If it is a story aimed simply at the local media, two or three press releases may be sufficient, sent to the reporter on the local evening paper and the local radio station.

Photographs and illustrations   Wherever possible, include a picture of the building or group of buildings that are at risk. There is no point in sending out actual photographs with every press release, but a clear photocopy will give the reporter a good idea of the building and may persuade his editor to send a photographer to take special pictures for the newspaper. Having said that, if you do have top-quality black and white photographs, then include one with the press releases to the national newspapers; they may want to carry the story but have no time to find a photograph themselves. Do not send valuable or irreplaceable photographs; if you put your name and address on the back, you may well get your print returned—but do not count on it!

Press conferences   At the national level, press conferences can often prove to be a waste of time and effort. Journalists can digest a story from a good press release in a few minutes, while attending a press conference is going to take an hour, not including travelling time. Of course if there is a very important issue, such as the launch of a major campaign, a press conference may be worthwhile. The judgment you have to make is Who will attend? The top reporters may not be able to spare the time and you could end up with the story being written by someone rather less familiar with the subject, whereas a quick telephone call or fax could mean that the story gets to the person you want.

At local level, a press conference can be very useful. A reporter's interest may be stimulated by attending an event, and you will have the chance to talk to him and gain a feel for his interest and views. Even if only two or three people from the media attend, it may be a good moment to organize an interview, making sure to flesh out the story with quotations from a range of people.

Press response   If there does not seem to be any response to your press release, do not be afraid to follow it up with a telephone call. Journalists do not mind being reminded so long as they do not think you are pressing them to write something they cannot be sure will be published. Once the media are interested, you and your fellow campaigners must make

WHAT YOU CAN DO

yourselves available for interviews and photographs. Most interviews, including radio, can be carried out on the telephone, with the reporter asking a few prepared questions. Try not to be nervous. Remember the most important thing is to get your message across clearly. Often the interviewer will need to play the devil's advocate, to put the other side's case forward. Reiterate the arguments in your press release calmly but firmly.

Be sure to cut out and keep all press cuttings. Circulate them as widely as possible. You can often get one of the national societies to write a rejoinder supporting your cause, which can be included in a dossier, together with notable letters and reports, for future use.

Local planners

Make immediate contact with the planning officers at your local planning authority (district or borough council). Find out who the personnel are and, in particular, who deals with conservation matters or listed building applications. Although conservation matters are generally assigned on an area basis, many councils now have their own conservation officers.

Go and see the plans for any new development if they have been lodged as a formal application.

If the proposals are particularly obnoxious, it may be that the developers and their architects refuse to provide any illustrations of plans suitable for publication. They may say that reproduction is a breach of copyright. Publishing excerpts from material such as planning applications for the purpose of public information, comment or criticism is not an infringement of copyright; alternatively, you could find someone who can make a reasonable but accurate sketch of the proposals.

Getting a building spotlisted

Lists of listed buildings are available for public inspection at the district council and county planning offices. Further copies may be held at the local public library. In addition, the Royal Commissions have complete sets of lists for England, Scotland and Wales.

The lists of listed buildings, though extensive, are often still far from comprehensive. The reason is simple. The criteria for listing have changed and broadened over the years to include more Victorian buildings and, subsequently, more twentieth-century buildings. Increased recognition is now given to the different interests of particular building types, such as Nonconformist chapels, railway stations, warehouses, hospitals and model housing.

The initial lists, for example, were compiled in a hurry and many of the more remote buildings were left out. There are many fine buildings—where a plain exterior conceals fine Georgian rooms, for example, or where there is an interesting timber-frame construction—that were also overlooked. Even if the list for an area has been revised fairly recently, the Department of the Environment may add a building to the list if there is new evidence about its interest or if it is an obvious omission.

SAVE ACTION GUIDE

Good photographs are likely to make all the difference to your submission. This does not mean expensive professional photography. Good colour snaps are fine as long as you get the building in focus, take it in sunlight rather than shadow and stand back far enough to ensure the whole building is in the picture. In addition, consider taking one or two photographs to show the building's immediate context. These will be useful in any event in explaining to people what the problem is and discussing what the possibilities of re-use are.

Historical information When you apply to have a building spotlisted you should supply details of its history if possible, and if time is available. For many buildings under threat there may be no obvious immediate source of information. Therefore talk to everybody who might know the building or have lived or worked there. Find out who owned it. Find a local historian or architect who can help you in dating or describing it.

Go to the local library and see if there are any old street guides or directories that include the building. Sometimes you can trace it back year by year or decade by decade to its construction.

Equally, the local library or county record office may have early maps or plans, which will provide a clue to the building's origin.

If the building was constructed in the last century, there is some possibility that the original planning application is still on file, complete with the architect's original drawings. This is particularly likely with commercial buildings or larger houses in residential suburbs. It may take some perseverance to get the appropriate files brought out of store, but it is well worthwhile.

Your application for listing the building should be sent to the Listing Branch, Department of the Environment, Lambeth Bridge House, Albert Embankment, London SE1 7SB. It will ask English Heritage to send an inspector to assess the building. The inspector makes a report and recommends whether or not to add the building to the statutory list. It is then up to the Secretary of State for the Environment (but more usually delegated to a junior minister or senior civil servant) to decide whether to accept the inspector's recommendation. You will be notified as to whether or not your application has been successful. The whole process is slow—perhaps a few months—but can be very quick in real emergencies.

It is a good idea to get some of the conservation bodies to write to the Department of the Environment supporting the listing application as well, particularly the Georgian Group or Victorian Society if the building falls within their remit.

Conservation area designation

Unlike the statutory listing of buildings, which is carried out by the Department of the Environment, it is local authorities that have the power to designate conservation areas. The legislation was introduced in 1966 under the Civic Amenities Bill by Duncan Sandys, founder of the Civic Trust. He felt that it was not enough merely to preserve isolated buildings,

WHAT YOU CAN DO

but that their setting should be protected and improved as well. The law defines conservation areas as 'areas of special architectural or historic interest, the character or appearance of which it is desirable to preserve or enhance'. Conservation area protection thus extends beyond buildings, to include streets, trees, paths and views.

The designation of these special areas is a vitally important way of protecting our heritage. There are thousands of buildings that despite being interesting and attractive—and perhaps important on a local scale—are not 'listable' in themselves; that is to say, they are not of sufficient architectural or historic interest to merit individual protection. And yet the loss of these buildings can really damage the character of a neighbourhood.

Conservation areas can be spread over large chunks of historic towns or just one street. They may encompass whole villages or a small hamlet in which there are just a scattering of modest but pretty cottages and a few barns.

To demolish any building within a conservation area, conservation area consent, like listed building consent, must be sought from the council. In determining the application, the planning committee must consider the contribution made by the building to the character of the area and whether its demolition would alter this. Similarly, any proposed redevelopment or new building must actively enhance or preserve the character or appearance of the conservation area.

Because conservation areas are designated by local authorities, they can be an effective way of protecting a building or group of buildings in danger. A 'tougher' form of protection for an area containing many buildings of historic interest, perhaps with particular features typical of the locality, comes when a local authority (with confirmation from the Department of the Environment) makes an Article 4 Direction. This means that specified alterations, from putting in new windows to removing chimney stacks, may not be carried out without consent. Article 4 Directions are particularly appropriate for model housing estates, railway villages, or the fine Georgian terraces of our spa towns.

Some local authorities have designated very few conservation areas. This may not necessarily mean the area has a scarcity of attractive buildings and open spaces. With a heavy workload and few specialized staff, for some councils conservation has taken second place. However, as with listing applications, any person can suggest an area for designation.

Try to get the support and interest of the planning officers who will be presenting the case to their committee. Prepare a brief report or booklet about the area—its history and any interesting information about the buildings it contains, some of which may already be listed. Take plenty of photographs, not just of individual buildings, but of their settings also—views down streets, through trees and across open spaces such as greens and commons. Be sure to include maps, current and historical ones if you can find them. Use your local library or record office.

Sometimes councils are reluctant to designate conservation areas if they feel the residents will object, but on the whole this is unlikely. Owners will usually see the value of their property increase and it is often a selling point in estate agents' particulars that a house stands in a conservation area. It is helpful to get the support and signatures of some of the residents.

Notify the press of your efforts to get a conservation area designated and send them a copy of the booklet you have prepared.

Establishing a trust

Quite a number of endangered buildings have been saved by local people who have set up a building preservation trust, acquired the building, restored it and sometimes resold it. Good guidance on this is included in information available from the Architectural Heritage Fund, 17 Carlton House Terrace, London SW1 5AW.

The Architectural Heritage Fund will be able to tell you whether there is already a local trust (perhaps a county trust) in existence. Quite often these trusts are on the lookout for new buildings to restore and may have some resources at their disposal. In any event, they should be able to provide you with good advice.

Do not, however, underestimate the problems you may encounter in taking on a building yourself. Delays in obtaining consents and grants can add considerably to the cost. It may be that the best solution is to find an individual or local entrepreneur who is enamoured of the building and willing and keen to make a first-class job of it.

Stopping the rot

Hundreds of historic buildings are standing empty and being allowed to decay. Prompt action by local people can not only prevent ultimate demolition, but also save many thousands of pounds in repair costs.

A blocked rainwater gutter leads very quickly to damp penetrating the walls. If the building is closed up and not properly ventilated, the perfect conditions for dry rot are likely to arise as soon as the weather gets warm.

Owners of listed buildings have a legal obligation to keep them in a reasonable state of repair. Local planning authorities, the Secretary of State and English Heritage all have powers to serve Repairs Notices. These notices take two main forms:

1. *A Section 101 Notice* This requires an owner to carry out urgent specified repairs; if he does not comply, then the council carries out the work and recovers the costs from the owner.

2. *A Section 114/115 Notice* This Repairs Notice can lead to compulsory purchase of a property by the planning authority if the repairs are not carried out.

For a long time, many local authorities were reluctant to use their repairs powers. They were afraid that owners might respond, as they are entitled to do, by serving a purchase order on the council. The council would thereby be obliged to purchase the building and in theory repair it at ratepayers' expense.

WHAT YOU CAN DO

Experience has shown that this virtually never happens. Usually an owner responds by placing the building on the market for the simple reason that most owners would rather sell to anyone than the local authority.

Very often a simple committee decision resolving to serve a Repairs Notice, or even resolving to consider serving a Repairs Notice, is enough to prompt the owner to sell.

It is important, none the less, to keep a careful watch on progress. Hard-worked planning officers may need encouragement to pursue the matter and find letters from concerned members of the public about neglected buildings a useful prompt to take the matter to their superiors or to their committee.

If the planning department is initially unwilling to consider Repairs Notices, then enlist the support of SAVE and the other societies, as appropriate, and ask English Heritage to consider taking action.

A local authority that has no previous experience of serving Repairs Notices can be encouraged in two ways. First, you could find someone who is interested in taking the building on should it be sold or ultimately come to compulsory purchase. Second, you, perhaps aided by SAVE or one of the other societies, could provide examples of similar cases that have been successfully resolved.

Legal action

One of SAVE's strongest suits has been the readiness, when other alternatives have been exhausted, to initiate legal action. Broadly there are three types of action a voluntary group can instigate:

1. *A writ of Mandamus*   This is an action requesting the court to require a minister—or local authority—to do what they are required to do by statute. For example, the Secretary of State for the Environment has a duty, not just a power, to compile lists of buildings of historic and architectural interest.

2. *A case of Ultra Vires*   This seeks to establish that a minister or local authority has acted beyond its powers.

3. *Leave for Judicial Review*   This requests the court to review and quash a decision by a minister or local authority.

Any discussion of legal action must be preceded by a caveat on costs. Lawsuits, as everyone knows, can prove very costly so it is preferable to seek to win your case by other means: by influencing public opinion, by making your case to officials and politicians, or by making representations at public inquiries. And the more you can show you have been closely involved in the battle from an early stage, the more weight you will carry if and when you decide to initiate legal action.

The first principle must be to obtain good advice. If possible find a solicitor or a barrister willing to advise you free of charge—perhaps out of office hours, when the meter is not ticking. If no such source is available, ask for a realistic estimate of potential costs on a stage by stage basis. Thus you will know what your liability is and can decide whether to proceed.

Second, be very wary of any type of action where you are likely to be required to give an undertaking on costs to the court.

If, for example, you obtain an injunction to halt building or demolition works, you may be interrupting a building contract; though this may well only be temporary, the opposition may also seek an undertaking, or even a bond, to cover their costs should you lose.

Wherever possible it is better to aim the action at local or central government for, say, failing to use their powers to stop the work. If you win, it will then be for them to serve an enforcement notice or injunction as appropriate. Moreover, the simple fact that court proceedings have been launched may halt the works.

If a fine building is in acute danger and the only way of saving it is immediate recourse to a judge-in-chambers for an injunction, be sure to find out what the potential costs will be. If a major contract is broken or delayed, they could be very high. However, much demolition is done on a piece work or per day basis, and you might simply be talking about the loss of a day's work or a day or two's profit.

In the first instance, a simple solicitor's letter may be sufficient to halt the work you wish to stop or to prompt action on a derelict building. Simplest of all is your own letter based on the advice of your lawyers, stating in formal legal terms the advice you have received and the action you intend to take if you do not receive a response. Where a building is under imminent threat or being callously neglected, voluntary organizations may be able to act more quickly than local authorities.

SAVE IN ACTION

Country Houses
Country House Parks
Gardens
Garden Buildings, Follies and Temples
Barns and Other Farm Buildings
Churches
Town Buildings
Interiors
Preserving Facades
Shopfronts
Street Furniture
Markets
Hospitals and Asylums
Industrial Buildings
Railway Stations and Structures
Pubs and Hotels
Theatres, Cinemas and Public Buildings
Public Parks

CAUSES AND CAMPAIGNS

THE FOLLOWING STUDIES and case histories are intended to show the strategy that SAVE has adopted towards different building types and owners. Again and again, we have found the key to the successful re-use of a building lies in its setting. While immediate surroundings may be derelict and depressing, once they are cleaned up and appropriately landscaped the appearance and appeal of the building is transformed.

Many owners, whether individuals or organizations, may initially see their redundant buildings simply as a burden and take the view that they have very little interest or merit. So the first need is to create awareness and recognition of a building's historical and architectural worth. Then, once the owner realizes that the building is of value, it may be possible to agree on a constructive course of action.

The examples of threatened buildings and open spaces covered in the next eighteen sections are just a very small selection of cases with which SAVE has been involved. Some buildings are larger and better known than others, and have had a great deal of publicity; others are perhaps more modest in both scale and workmanship, but still deserving of attention as an important part of the local scene. We hope that by including a variety of cases we can inspire individuals and groups all over the country to take up arms on behalf of a threatened building in their neighbourhood.

① COUNTRY HOUSES

ENDANGERED COUNTRY HOUSES fall principally into three categories:
1. Country houses that substantially retain their contents and collections and are candidates for preservation intact as showpieces.
2. Country houses that have lost their contents and are empty and even abandoned.
3. Country houses in institutional use that are under threat of closure and in urgent need of a new owner and a new use.

Country houses have often been described as 'collective works of art' and as one of Britain's greatest contributions to the visual arts. The need is to safeguard not only their architecture, interiors and gardens, but also their wider setting; and hard experience shows that the prospect of finding a secure, viable, long-term use for these houses diminishes dramatically as their setting is eroded.

All decisions on country houses in Britain need to be taken against the background of the massive destruction over the past hundred years, which reached a climax in 1955. For the Victoria and Albert exhibition, 'The Destruction of the Country House', Peter Reid compiled a list of more than 1,200 houses that had been demolished in the preceding century. Subsequent research suggests that the probable total of demolitions is nearer double that figure. This, in turn, suggests that between one quarter and one third of all country seats that existed in 1875 have been demolished.

Country houses with their contents

Over the last fifteen years, successive governments have taken the view that the best way to preserve great houses is to make it possible for their traditional owners to maintain them. When Capital Transfer Tax was introduced in 1975 substantial exemptions were granted for outstanding historic houses, their contents and amenity land (and provisions made for maintenance funds) in return for public access and undertakings for

Demolished country houses

above left *Spixworth Hall, Norfolk;* **below left** *Paxton Park, Cambridgeshire;* **opposite above left** *Henham Hall, Suffolk;* **above right** *Carter Place Hall, Lancashire;* **centre left** *Tranby Lodge, Humberside;* **centre right** *Baynards Park, Surrey;* **below** *Billing Hall, Northamptonshire*

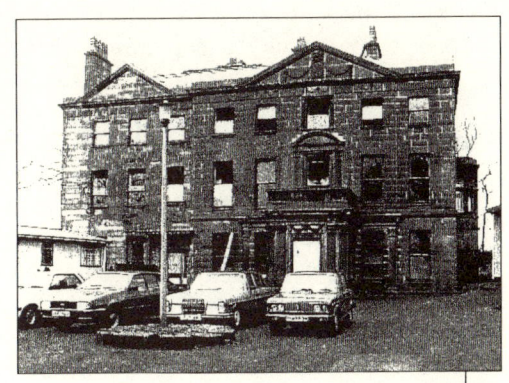

conservation. As a result, virtually every great house in Britain is regularly open to the public, as are numerous small manor houses.

However, the cost of repairs, lack of heirs and financial or family problems inevitably mean that every two or three years a great house faces sale and break-up. Since SAVE was established in 1975, these have included Mentmore Towers in Buckinghamshire, Belton House, Lincolnshire, Kedleston Hall and Calke Abbey in Derbyshire, Thoresby Hall, Nottinghamshire, and Brodsworth Hall, South Yorkshire. At the smaller end of the scale, the surreal Monkton House in West Sussex and the delightful sixteen-sided folly at A la Ronde outside Exmouth in Devon have also come under threat.

The natural solution in such cases is to look to the National Trust or the National Trust for Scotland. The problem of course is that, even if the Trusts are given house, contents and land, they need a major endowment to ensure preservation in perpetuity. From their own experience of endowments that have proved inadequate, the National Trust has evolved a method of calculation known as the 'Chorley formula'. This aims to produce an annual income looking fifty years ahead which must be sufficient to make up the operating deficit.

Brodsworth Hall, South Yorkshire. A great Victorian house with remarkable contents will be preserved intact and opened to the public by English Heritage

COUNTRY HOUSES

One of the major changes that came with the creation of the National Heritage Memorial Fund from the National Land Fund was that the Fund was empowered to provide endowments (see also page 42). Since then several major houses have been secured for the National Trust in this way, notably Belton, Calke and Kedleston.

In these circumstances, it is the preservation not only of a great house that is assured, but also of the surrounding area of countryside. The Trusts, with their concern for public access and amenity, and increasingly for conservation-conscious farming and forestry, as well as for the protection of wildlife, will ensure that large areas of land are maintained to high standards of conservation. Hedges will be maintained and hedgerow trees replanted; use of chemicals will be reduced; and old farms, cottages and barns will be repaired. In looking at the size of endowments for these houses it is important to recognize the wider benefits that are secured.

The National Heritage Memorial Fund has also set out to encourage the creation of individual charitable trusts for such houses. These can work particularly well where a strong family involvement continues. Arundel Castle in West Sussex is preserved by such a trust, so is Leeds Castle in Kent. Arundel, as the seat of England's premier duke, the Duke of Norfolk, also has the support of an exceptional number of visitors; and Leeds was munificently endowed by the late Lady Bailey. The Fund has been able to assist with new charitable trusts at Thirlestane and Newliston in Lothian.

Continuing family involvement means that the endowment may be considerably smaller. It may be needed simply, for example, for the part of the house containing the main staterooms. While individual trusts are to be encouraged, their success in the long term depends on the continuing level of commitment, and above all drive, on the part of the trustees. Where an owner continues to be centrally involved and lives in the house or on the estate, attitudes are likely to be positive and the house opened in a lively fashion. There are other cases where such trusts are in danger of becoming sleepy animals, only barely keeping up with the minimum requirement to provide public access.

The establishment of English Heritage opened up the possibility of a second refuge for endangered houses, capable—at least in theory—of taking houses on without the massive endowments required by the National Trust. English Heritage, it was argued, could pay the annual deficit from its own annual grant from the government. But so far only Brodsworth has been taken in this way and the signs are that English Heritage, which is under severe financial pressure, is not likely to take on many, if any, further houses.

Much discussion revolves round whether English Heritage (whose 400 castles and abbeys are largely unfurnished) has the capacity to care for fragile interiors and furniture in the same way as the National Trust. The quality of advice provided by English Heritage on the restoration of

SAVE ACTION GUIDE

Frogmore House, where Queen Charlotte lived, in Windsor Great Park, shows that it does have very considerable expertise in this area. While the National Trust must be the number one choice for great houses, the existence of alternatives with a different approach can only be healthy.

Controversy really begins when there are varying views as to whether a house is worth saving. While the case for Belton and Kedleston had near-universal support, Mentmore and Calke both had their detractors. The curator of the Jeffery Museum scorned Mentmore as no more than 'a heterogeneous accumulation of prestigious loot', while Lord Vaizey scathingly described the contents of Calke as 'skiploads of junk'.

The important point here is that country houses are not simply art galleries or museums, of value purely for their great paintings and furniture; they also provide a remarkable document of numerous aspects of life and work over several centuries. In the past, when houses were accepted as payment for death duties, the selection of the contents acquired with them tended to be made mainly on a museum-oriented scale of value, concentrating predominantly on items that were not only of high quality, but also usually an integral part of the design of a room. As a result, many of these houses not only lost their lived-in feel, but were also emptied of the everyday objects that are increasingly seen as essential to a proper understanding of their history and function.

In North America, emphasis is now placed not only on art history but also on what is termed 'material culture'—that is, everything pertaining to the lives and activities of all those who lived in the house. The importance of Calke was that (as at Erddig in North Wales) everything in the house was on offer. Better still, very little had ever been thrown away.

While some may come to admire the Guercino or the girandoles, many people, including children, may enjoy looking at the old or not-so-old toys, or even a collection of fifty years of milk bottles from the local dairy. And among the unexpected discoveries in the 'skiploads of junk' at Calke was a state bed with all its Chinese hangings, which had never been unwrapped and was therefore in mint condition (valued at £1 million at least).

Another problem arises when two houses that are close in date or place come under threat at the same time. The question Which is the more important? is asked, suggesting one house only should be saved and the other relinquished. SAVE has faced this dilemma with Kedleston and Calke, and subsequently with Thoresby and Brodsworth. However, to forsake one building for the benefit of another can result in the loss of both. Precisely this happened in the case of two churches by Bassett Keeling, which both came under threat in the 1970s. The first was passed by with a view to concentrating efforts on the second. But the loss of one simply paved the way for the loss of the other.

SAVE's view is that the case for preserving any building must be judged on its own merit. No-one can predict how events will unfold. The future of Kedleston was uncertain for at least a decade. While it was unquestionably

COUNTRY HOUSES

the most important candidate for saving by the nation, if all efforts had been concentrated on it to the exclusion of others the nation would have lost Belton and Calke.

Most thinking on the preservation of houses revolves round major aristocratic seats or ancient manor houses. More thought needs to be given to finding and preserving examples of more modest farmhouses and cottages, and even a particularly characteristic 'semi' in the London suburbs or a Glasgow tenement. A show flat is preserved in this way in the Karl Marx Hof in Vienna.

The problem with these 'lowlier' buildings is that when they come under threat they rarely make the news. They may owe their intact status to the fact that they belong to a recluse. For this reason discovery and awareness depends on local people. So if ever you hear of such period pieces please get in touch with SAVE.

Case History
MENTMORE TOWERS, BUCKINGHAMSHIRE

EARLY IN 1977, SAVE was faced with one of its greatest challenges—the break-up of the great Rosebery Collection at Mentmore Towers in Buckinghamshire. The future of Mentmore had been discussed behind bolted doors since the death of the sixth Earl of Rosebery. The new Lord Rosebery was faced with a large bill for death duties and the choice between Mentmore and the family's beautiful house at Dalmeny on the Firth of Forth.

The Government was unwilling to spend money on taking over the house, but for a long time courted various businessmen in the hope that they would provide a major part of the funds. SAVE first heard of the danger of a possible sale in September and immediately issued a press release:

> Whitehall procrastination may soon result in the break-up of one of Britain's outstanding stately homes. This is Mentmore in Buckinghamshire, built in 1852–54 by Sir Joseph Paxton (designer of the Crystal Palace) for Baron Meyer Amschel de Rothschild. His daughter married the Earl of Rosebery to whose descendants the house belongs. The sixth Lord Rosebery died in 1974, and his heir, faced with massive death duties, has offered Mentmore, its grounds, and its priceless contents to the Government in settlement of his liabilities. There are several precedents for the Government accepting stately homes in payment of death duties: examples are Petworth Park, Sussex, Sudbury Hall, Derbyshire, Tatton Park, Cheshire, and Saltram Park, Devon.
>
> If the Government refuses to accept the house, then Lord Rosebery must auction the contents. If this has to be done it must be (for

SAVE ACTION GUIDE

SAVE

MENTMORE FOR THE NATION

Mentmore Towers, Buckinghamshire. Family financial problems and Whitehall procrastination jeopardized the future of one of the finest ensembles of Victorian taste. SAVE produced a leaflet, **above**, *within a few days as part of its campaign. The postcard,* **right**, *also helped to raise public awareness*

technical reasons) within three years of his father's death—by 30 May 1977. To catalogue and prepare a major sale will take months. It is even rumoured that the end of September is the deadline for the Government's decision.

Mentmore contains, after the Wallace Collection and Waddesdon, the finest collection of eighteenth-century French furniture in England—one of the best in the world. The contents also form a unique ensemble of Victorian taste. SAVE believes that Mentmore and all its contents should be acquired for the nation and handed to the Victoria and Albert Museum. What could be more appropriate than for it to take on a great nineteenth-century house to complement the seventeenth- and eighteenth-century interiors at Ham and Osterley?

The Government resolutely refused to comment until in January 1978 we suddenly heard that an exasperated Lord Rosebery had broken off the sale and given Sotheby's the go-ahead to auction the contents in May.

SAVE reacted with a lightning leaflet, *SAVE Mentmore for the Nation*, publishing the first photographs of the magnificent interiors and describing in detail the remarkable furnishings. Lord Rosebery responded quickly by saying that he would still sell to the nation, but was increasing the price from £2 to £3 million for the house and contents. This was to prove a bargain offer as the contents alone were later to be sold for £6 million. Although the increase was understandable given the Government's vacillation, it made ministers even less willing to intervene.

In one sense, Mentmore was a lost cause even before we began. Academic opinion was divided as to the merits of the house; and Lady

Save Mentmore for the Nation

SAVE ACTION GUIDE

Birk, the minister involved, was constantly to refer to 'other voices' who whispered behind closed doors that the house was not worth saving. But the outcome was to demonstrate forcefully that you should never shy away from a fight for fear of losing. Not only may a campaign raise public awareness of the issues involved and win you new supporters, but the sheer relentlessness of pressure and eventual embarrassment at being seen to do nothing may also prompt Parliament or Government to introduce new policies.

Our campaign soon led us to investigate the finances of the National Land Fund, which over the previous twenty years had been used to acquire a whole series of country houses for the nation.

The National Land Fund, we discovered from a reluctant Treasury press officer, stood at £17 million, but the income from the capital was subject to an expenditure ceiling of £2 million divided equally between the Department of the Environment and the Department of Education and Science.

Why, we asked innocently, could not the allocation from the two Departments be put together to match the £2 million original asking price for Mentmore? The Department of the Environment would pay largely for the building and the Department of the Education and Science for the works of art, reflecting their respective spheres of responsibility. No, no, we were told, the Department of Education and Science had numerous other potential commitments and could never commit its entire allocation to one collection.

Now we went on the attack. The National Land Fund had been set up in 1946 as the nation's war memorial. Dr Dalton, the Chancellor of the Exchequer, had put £50 million from the sale of surplus war stores into the Fund so that outstanding land could be purchased as a 'thank-offering for victory'.

Such was the momentum—and even anger—aroused by our campaign that, shortly after the auction took place, the House of Commons Environment Committee mounted a special inquiry into the National Land Fund. And when the report was published, the Committee adopted our central recommendation—which went further than virtually everyone else who gave evidence—that the National Land Fund should be reconstituted under independent trustees. To our delight the National Land Fund was recreated as the National Heritage Memorial Fund on 1 April 1980.

The guidelines issued to the National Heritage Memorial Fund allowed it to give grants, not only for the purchase of outstanding buildings, land and works of artistic and historic interest, but also to provide endowments for major houses threatened with sale.

In the past, such houses had always been offered to the National Trust, which had initially taken them without endowment, accepting instead an undertaking that the Ministry of Works would make good any deficit on repairs and maintenance through a Historic Buildings

COUNTRY HOUSES

Council grant. This system was proving so unsatisfactory that the National Trust had declared it would take no further houses unless endowments could be provided. Following the creation of the National Heritage Memorial Fund, several outstanding houses have been saved with their contents and handed to the National Trust.

Case History
THORESBY HALL, NOTTINGHAMSHIRE

THE SAD SAGA of Thoresby is a cautionary tale. Built in 1864–71, Thoresby was one of the famous Nottinghamshire 'Dukeries' that 100 years ago made up the most illustrious group of houses in Britain. Worksop Manor and Clumber Park had long since disappeared and Welbeck Abbey had become a military training school. Thoresby was the only one to survive, with the majority of its contents still on display in the staterooms, regularly opened to the public.

But though the contents still belonged to the family trustees, the house had been sold to British Coal. In 1980, mining operations threatened the fabric of the house and British Coal, calculating it would be cheaper to cope with subsidence problems if it owned the house itself, acquired the property. As the future was so uncertain, however, the family retained

Thoresby Hall, Nottinghamshire. A nineteenth-century photograph shows how little the opulent interior had changed, with much of the original furnishing still in situ

ownership of all fixtures, fittings and moveable contents—everything that could be stripped out if Thoresby were ever threatened with demolition.

The mining never took place. Instead, the Coal Board, by now reconstituted as British Coal, decided to sell the building. This precipitated the sale of the contents.

There was a strong case for saving Thoresby for the nation, but unfortunately its future came into question just at the moment when all thoughts were focused on Brodsworth, near Doncaster, another Victorian house with an even more complete set of contents. Everyone was agreed that Brodsworth was the most remarkable of all surviving mid-Victorian interiors and Thoresby, for all its impressiveness, suffered as a result.

Once it became clear that there was no possiblity of raising the funds for the National Trust or English Heritage to take on the house, SAVE began to look at other options. British Coal had decided to sell the house for conversion into a hotel to Roo Management, a company run by an Australian businessman who had also bought Holme Lacey in Herefordshire with the intention of making it a hotel. In the circumstances, hotel use was clearly a good second best, as it meant that the staterooms could be used for functions and so still seen by the public.

This, however, was the nub of the problem. The family was willing in principle to loan or sell some of the most important contents of the staterooms to a hotel, but only on condition that they were given proper conservation safeguards. This meant, for example, that no smoking would be allowed and the use of the blue drawing room would have to be on an occasional basis. Roo Management wanted to put these rooms to intensive use throughout the day and in these circumstances it was clear that the contents could not remain. British Coal, however, had received an alternative offer from a local Nottinghamshire businessman, Mr C. G. Whitaker, who was proposing a mixture of uses for the house—as a hotel and flats—while retaining the staterooms for public viewing and small-scale corporate meetings.

SAVE published *The Plundering of Thoresby Hall*, which was an extensively documented and well-illustrated description of the contents of the house. This showed conclusively that Thoresby's contents were far more complete than had previously been realized and, with relatively little rearrangement, could have been put back as they appeared in early photographs. From this research it was clear that Thoresby Hall, properly displayed, could have been an altogether exceptional and highly interesting document of the taste of the time.

British Coal, however, remained adamant that the Roo Management offer alone was acceptable, and proceeded to sell the house to the company. Thoresby's contents were duly auctioned or removed and a major historic ensemble was completely dispersed. Mr Tondut of Roo Management expressed outrage at the difficulties conservationists caused him and was quoted in the national press as saying, 'I

COUNTRY HOUSES

don't want to do anything to damage these houses. I want to give them back their life.'

However, when Roo Management obtained the necessary planning permissions for conversion to a hotel, it did not proceed with the conversion but simply put the house on the market; and the house has been bought by none other than Mr Whitaker, the very man who wanted to keep the staterooms intact.

British Coal, in proceeding as it did, failed to secure the responsible and appropriate use of the house it had promised. This was a disgraceful dereliction of duty. The Coal Board had originally purchased the house to ensure its preservation. When it did this the family had been on the point of vesting the house in a charitable trust, which would have secured its future complete with contents. As it was, British Coal's intervention led needlessly to the break up of one of the last surviving High Victorian ensembles in England.

Empty and abandoned country houses

Over the last fifteen years, SAVE has been continuously involved in campaigning to secure the future of disused, decaying and neglected country houses. A series of reports have illustrated and catalogued several hundred of these houses.

Silent Mansions. *A SAVE report on threatened country houses published in 1981. Within three years over one third had found new owners or uses*

SAVE ACTION GUIDE

The Lost Houses of Wales

In 1985, we were approached by Tom Lloyd, a young solicitor from Carmarthen with a passion for historic buildings—particularly, of course, those of Wales. He pointed out to us, quite rightly, that the celebrated 'Destruction of the Country House' exhibition had illustrated just a fraction of Welsh losses and no extensive record of demolished country houses in the Principality had ever been published. He showed us the research he had begun in Pembrokeshire, and we were so amazed at what he had discovered that we encouraged him to continue all over Wales.

As a result, *The Lost Houses of Wales* was published in 1986 and caused a massive stir with extensive press coverage. Tom became an overnight celebrity. The SAVE office was flooded with inquiries and orders, and it seemed that every village post office wanted to stock it. We sold out within three months and have reprinted it twice.

What the book set out to show was that Wales had, for its size, as fine a legacy of country houses and estates as England. Many had been demolished, burnt down or left to run to ruin, leaving only the more modest farmhouses and other traditional vernacular buildings normally associated with the Welsh countryside.

In the first edition, a chapter was included on some fine houses still standing, but empty and at risk. Two years later, by the time the second edition was published, most of these had been rescued and were off the danger list.

Ynysymaengwyn, Gwynedd, **above**, *and Pontysgaryd, Powys,* **right**, *are demolished houses illustrated in* The Lost Houses of Wales, *1986*

COUNTRY HOUSES

The acquisition and painstaking restoration of Plas Teg, an exceptionally beautiful early seventeenth-century house in Clwyd, was a brave step for the private individual who took on the house with the help of grants. And it has inspired similar projects. Llangoed Hall, a most romantic house built in 1912 by Sir Clough Williams-Ellis, in a wonderful setting beside the River Wye in Powys, lay empty for fifteen years but has recently opened as a first-class country house hotel. The sheer impact of *The Lost Houses of Wales* had really brought home the message.

Empty Quarters

Towards the end of 1988 many people were asking: Are there still any buildings at risk? Haven't you saved them all? We knew, from our travels around the country, that there were many buildings standing empty and derelict, and we decided to start a register, firstly to try to assess the scale of the problem and secondly to try to foster interest in their repair and restoration.

A letter was sent out to every planning authority asking whether there were any empty listed buildings in its district that would benefit from some publicity. We had a flood of cases: buildings of all types and sizes, of all styles and ages, but with one thing in common—they were disused and decaying and evidently in need of a new owner or a new use, as their present owners were being decidedly neglectful. Of course, the response

SAVE ACTION GUIDE

Lifford Hall near Birmingham. This seventeenth-century house, after appearing in SAVE's report Empty Quarters, *was successfully converted into offices*

varied from council to council. Some said they had no listed buildings at risk at all, others that there were so many their hands were full and they had no time to reply.

We published the results of our survey in spring 1989. A lengthy article appeared in the *Daily Telegraph* entitled 'Would you like to live in a listed ruin?'; then pieces appeared in all the rest of the newspapers. The office was bombarded by telephone calls, letters and visitors. We had always known that there were many people looking for a historic biilding to restore but had not realized the extent, which was very encouraging.

Two years later, we published a second edition, *Nobody's Home*, for which demand was even higher. Planning officers were keen to contribute once more, as our report clearly helped the situation. As one planner told SAVE, 'A few letters from potential purchasers asking about a neglected listed building gives me the necessary ammunition to persuade my council to serve a Repairs Notice on the owner.' Many of the cases included in the two reports are now on the road to recovery.

The Lost and Endangered Houses of Scotland
The cold facts and figures of country houses and castles demolished in Scotland—over 400 this century—were described by John Harris in his introduction to SAVE's 1980 report, *The Lost Houses of Scotland*, as demonstrating 'the awful scale of the Scottish calamity . . . the quality of what has been lost is mind-boggling.'

COUNTRY HOUSES

Exactly ten years later, and somewhat sadly, a different report was compiled, *Scotland's Endangered Houses*. These houses (140 were identified and illustrated) still stand, but are neglected and decaying and in desperate need of new owners and new uses. Scotland has evidently not learnt a lesson from what it has lost.

The second SAVE publication sent shock waves through the country. As with all the SAVE reports on country houses, public interest has been immense. There has been a reaction almost of incredulity that so many really beautiful buildings—some in splendid settings—are going to waste.

Scotland's Endangered Houses. *A report on 140 deserted country houses and castles*

SAVE ACTION GUIDE

The good news is that usually two thirds of the houses illustrated in any one report—these include *Tomorrow's Ruins*, *Silent Mansions*, *Endangered Domains* and *Vanishing Houses of England*—have found new owners or new uses within two years of publication. Indeed, such is the degree of interest in substantial properties offered for sale that the nature of the problem has changed, and a new threat has appeared as developers promise to restore houses if only they can be given planning permission for extensive new building.

Repeated cases have convinced SAVE that allowing permission for development in the grounds of country houses must be strongly resisted. Not only does development of this kind damage the setting, it very often fails to produce the promised restoration.

Sir William Chambers' beautiful Palladian villa at Duddingston on the outskirts of Edinburgh is a tragic example. Here permission was given for the construction of a large courtyard development of twenty-six houses and flats, quite out of character with the compact eighteenth-century house, in the belief that the profits yielded from the sale of the flats would go back into the house. To ensure this happened, permission for phase II of the development, a further twenty-eight flats, was not to be given until the house had been restored.

But it has not happened this way. Instead, the Chambers villa has been sold on separately to a local construction company. The original plan to restore the house as a hotel has lapsed and new proposals have been lodged with the city council for dividing the house into flats with new front doors set randomly into many of the original window frames, and with no use for the spectacular hall and staircase.

As soon as there is any prospect of allowing planning permission, all that usually happens is that the price of the house is bid up far beyond what it is worth, given the large sums that need to be spent on it. If a commercial buyer pays over the odds, obtaining planning permission becomes an ever more important part of the financial equation, and while the argument rages the house continues to rot.

Herstmonceux Castle in East Sussex is a parallel case. Here, the English Tourist Board and the local authority decided the magnificent fifteenth-century castle, if it was to remain intact and open to the public, would not find a purchaser without permission for development. Hence the concept devised—and now enshrined in the local plan—for adding a major wing to the castle just across the moat, effectively doubling the size of the castle. Additionally, provision for sixty timeshare units in the grounds was written into the local plan.

The house was afterwards acquired by a company, James Developments, which developed the scheme in considerable detail and obtained letters of approval in principle from the local authority. However, as timeshare was getting a bad name, the holiday cottages grew into sixty corporate lodges aimed at attracting Japanese purchasers.

COUNTRY HOUSES

Herstmonceux Castle, East Sussex. An expensive set of particulars was produced to promote the potential for a controversial development within the grounds

The house was then advertised for sale at £15 million compared to the £6 million it had sold for in 1988. Happily, Herstmonceux has not been sold to a corporate buyer seeking to take advantage of this potential cornucopia of planning permissions, but to an American who values the place for its beauty and history.

Local authorities, English Heritage, and ministers and their advisors must be made aware that giving planning permission to build in the grounds of houses does not lead automatically to their restoration. The more usual outcome is that the house is simply re-advertised for sale with the benefit of the planning permission.

Too many decaying country houses belong to non-resident owners who are reluctant to sell. It may be that they simply see no value in the building or that they are concerned that any use of the building might detract from their estate or business. Houses have been bought by local builders with plans to restore them, though in many such cases very little work is actually done. Some owners are convinced that their properties, even in an extremely derelict state, are worth a major sum and price the building out of the market.

If it is clear that a listed building is being neglected and is in urgent need of repair, and the owner has no plans to remedy this or to sell the property, the next stage is simple. The local planning authority, English Heritage or the Secretary of State must use their powers to serve a Repairs Notice.

SAVE ACTION GUIDE

The owner may contest the Repairs Notice because he is determined not to relinquish ownership. The two most prolonged battles of this kind, at Mavisbank near Edinburgh and Pell Wall in Shropshire, are cases where the owners have been deaf to every offer to take on the house and restore it.

Case History
THE GRANGE, HAMPSHIRE

ONE OF SAVE's strongest suits has been the readiness, when all other alternatives have been exhausted, to resort to legal action.

The first case which SAVE took up in this way was The Grange in Hampshire. This great neoclassical house had been reprieved from imminent demolition in 1972 by ministers and taken into guardianship two years later. Over the next four years, no work of any kind was carried out and it became increasingly apparent that senior officials had decided that The Grange should not be restored after all. They were therefore leaving it exposed to the elements until it reached the point where ministers decided it was a waste of time and money to restore it.

Prolonged correspondence with the Department of the Environment revealed that there were no plans for restoration. SAVE obtained a copy of the guardianship deed. We found that ministers had solemnly undertaken not only to repair The Grange, but also to open it to the public.

Our solicitors, therefore, wrote to the Department of the Environment informing them that we were considering seeking judicial review of

The Grange, Hampshire. Neglected by the Department of the Environment, only the threat of legal action stopped the decay. It is now well cared for and open to the public

the case. Soon after, we received a telephone call requesting us to attend a meeting at the Department with the Head of the Directorate of Ancient Monuments and Historic Buildings. We were told, of course, that if only a little more time could be provided a satisfactory solution might emerge. But winter was coming on and our fear was that The Grange would suffer further grievous damage. We agreed to a limited extension on the basis that we would have to show the court that we had provided reasonable opportunity for the Department to consider the matter.

From this time, we began to build up pressure on the Department, first on a weekly then on an almost daily basis, until eventually we heard that ministers had decided to fulfil the undertakings in the guardianship deed.

The writ was never served, but it was perfectly clear that without aggressive and persistent action by our solicitors the Department would have continued to stall indefinitely.

Case History
PELL WALL HALL, MARKET DRAYTON, SHROPSHIRE

THIS WAS THE last country house designed by one of Britain's greatest architects, Sir John Soane, in 1822. Despite its importance and grade II* listing, the treatment it has received in recent years has been disgraceful, and it is to be hoped a great many lessons will have been learnt about how to deal with irresponsible owners of such important listed buildings. After many attempts by the owner to demolish Pell Wall, with three public inquiries—each refusing permission—then a serious fire in 1987, North Shropshire District Council finally managed to compulsorily purchase the building from the owner. The price was £1—hardly worth the owner's protracted fight! Though now a shell, having been stabilized by the British Historic Buildings Trust, Pell Wall still offers great potential for a number of uses. Someone with imagination and funds might wish to recreate the villa to Soane's original designs. Alternatively, office or hotel use may be suitable.

Country houses that have been in institutional use

Many of the country houses requisitioned during the Second World War never returned to domestic use. Instead, they were taken over for institutional use, sometimes in a public-spirited move to give them a new lease of life, sometimes for exploitation as large areas of relatively cheap floor space.

Numerous houses became schools, many more became hospitals and quite a number were acquired as reform schools. The most successful perhaps were those acquired as teacher training colleges, such as Wentworth Castle and Wentworth Woodhouse which, without such use, might not have survived at all.

SAVE ACTION GUIDE

Pell Wall Hall, Shropshire. Gutted by fire but not beyond saving. A new owner is sought with the means to restore this, Sir John Soane's last country house

Experience shows that most forms of institutional use follow a remarkably clear pattern. First, the institution needs more floor space and begins to build in the grounds. The earliest extensions or additions may be discreetly sited and carefully designed, but very quickly the hut syndrome is underway and the house is rapidly surrounded by one- or two-storey flat-roofed extensions of the very utilitarian kind mercilessly caricatured by Osbert Lancaster.

Then, with dramatic abruptness, a decision is taken to close the institution or move on. It may be that the old building needs major repairs. The standards and safety measures now required for the care of the elderly and disabled mean that houses used, for example, as Cheshire Homes, can only be brought up to current standards at inordinate expense and involving radical alteration of the historic interiors. It may be part of departmental cuts or administrative reorganization. Again and again, users, after a period of about fifteen years, suddenly decide to leave. Often this is the best thing for the building. Many of these houses have reached the point where further extensions would completely overwhelm them.

The challenge then is to find a new use which will not only secure the future of the house but undo some of the damage that has been done.

If the huts are relatively few and insubstantial, then the best solution will be to demolish them and reinstate the gardens and grounds. One of the best examples where this has happened is the restoration of Hartwell House in Buckinghamshire. Formerly a school, it has been converted into a country house hotel by Richard Broyd, following on from his earlier conversion of Middlethorpe Hall on the edge of York. Today, Middlethorpe shows no signs of its hard years of institutional use.

There are, however, some houses where the institutional additions are just too substantial to demolish, or represent an investment that will prompt someone to offer a higher price. The pretty eighteenth-century Gothick villa of Stout's Hill near Stroud was a small house much extended while a school. The gymnasium, swimming pool and even classrooms have been given a new lease of life as part of a timeshare development—such facilities having been a positive attraction to buyers. Timeshare is not normally a solution SAVE would recommend for a historic house because so much of the expenditure goes on pure marketing, leaving too little for the building, but where it is well organized the outcome may be satisfactory.

Problems arise when an institution—particularly a government department or a hospital—is offered for sale with the carrot of planning permission to build in the grounds. Estate agents' advertisements habitually claim that country houses are suitable for every use from country clubs to prestige headquarters. But when a building looks a problem to sell, some planning authorities show a dangerous tendency to try to be kind and make encouraging noises that parts of the grounds might be suitable for development. This must be resisted. New houses may be built, but more often than not they compromise the setting of the house without generating funds to restore it.

In such situations, the most vital point is to resist any kind of planning application for development that will fragment the grounds—for example, permission to build houses in a walled garden which can (and will) be sold off as a separate development. Multiple residential schemes work well only when they involve a total plan for the grounds and setting of a house, and provide for their continued upkeep. The pioneer of this kind of approach is Kit Martin, who has successfully rescued and converted a series of great country houses including Dingley in Northamptonshire, Gunton in Norfolk, Callaly in Northumberland and most recently Tyninghame in East Lothian. SAVE has been closely involved at the early stages of two more, The Hazells in Bedfordshire and Cullen House in Banffshire, both of which were under serious threat.

Kit Martin emphasizes strongly that he makes houses not flats. In each property these range from houses with five to six bedrooms or more—the size of a rectory or Scottish tower house—to two-bedroom cottages in the service wings or stables. This solution works particularly well in houses which have evolved over several centuries, where it is possible to repair a wing at a time, selling the houses as they near completion and recycling the investment. His conversions involve few external visible alterations or internal subdivision of rooms. Most people, he finds, posivitely enjoy having one or two large grand rooms and, since the main staterooms in these houses tend to be on one floor, they can be apportioned between the individual houses.

He makes a point of acquiring a substantial area of grounds, not just the lawns immediately around the house, but the walled gardens and shrubberies beyond, running to twenty or even fifty acres. Communally maintained for the benefit of all the residents, the setting of the house remains unchanged with a certainty that it will be looked after on a continuing basis. Gardens are only apportioned individually where there is a clear self-contained entity, such as a walled garden or, say, a rose garden laid out formally in front of a wing. In addition he seeks covenants to ensure that surrounding parkland remains as pasture so that the wider country house landscape is assured protection.

A special problem is presented by former country houses engulfed by urban sprawl. Often the grounds of such houses were acquired as much-needed public parks (or indeed bequeathed as such by their owners). Often these houses were used initially as museums, but eventually fell victim to a series of expenditure cutbacks. Examples are Danson Hill near Bexleyheath, Highcliffe Castle in Dorset, Hylands near Chelmsford, Grovelands in North London, Oak Hill Mansion in Accrington, Lancashire, and Callendar House near Falkirk in Scotland.

In such cases there is a reluctance to part with the house except on impossible terms: on a short lease or without any land to give it a moderate degree of privacy; or there may be restrictions on the uses that are allowed—community uses only, perhaps, to be financed from public funds, which are not forthcoming.

The first need in such cases is to make a convincing case for the importance of the house, not only in architectural terms, but as the centrepiece of the park landscape. What is at stake is not the creation of a private zone in a public place, but the restoration of a local facility which everyone can enjoy.

The house must be offered for sale on a long lease—which means 125 years—with its immediate gardens and shrubberies: the area, roughly speaking, within the ha-ha, together with the drive.

The most successful example of a solution along these lines is Grovelands, in which SAVE was closely involved. It cannot be too strongly stressed that people who use public parks enjoy seeing the building that was once its raison d'être. Conversely, if the house is demolished the layout of the park loses its main feature and is likely to become more and more ragged.

For all the rough treatment meted out to houses in institutional use, many retain remarkably fine interiors. The furniture and furnishings may be wholly unsuitable; partitions and fire doors may have caused considerable damage—but the houses themselves remain, in architectural terms, of the highest importance. The architectural historian Mark Girouard pointed out that, but for the institution of the English public school, virtually no

COUNTRY HOUSES

great Victorian house would survive. Such houses may have lost their furniture and collections, but they retain remarkable plasterwork and woodwork, fine halls, staircases and saloons, marble chimneypieces and mahogany doors.

Case History
NUTFIELD PRIORY, REIGATE, SURREY

NUTFIELD PRIORY, AN enormous Victorian Gothic mansion near Reigate, had for many years been a school for the blind. The huge proportions of the main rooms made it unsuitable for conversion into houses, as did the flat-roofed additions—albeit designed with some care. The house is now a hotel, catering for local weddings and business receptions; and the school sports facilities, including the covered pool, have been integrated as an attraction for people wanting an active weekend. It may not have three red roofs in the Michelin guide, but anyone who likes to dine beneath soaring Gothic vaults will find it a memorable experience.

Case History
BARLASTON HALL, STAFFORDSHIRE

SAVE'S PURCHASE OF Barlaston Hall for £1 is now legendary. The deal took place at a public inquiry in 1981, when the owner, Wedgwood, was applying for a second time for consent to demolish.

Wedgwood had acquired the Barlaston estate in the 1930s, moving their whole operation there from Josiah Wedgwood's original site at Etruria. The new factory was built on the far side of the property, leaving Barlaston surveying a fine sweep of parkland down to a river widened to look like a lake.

Initially, Barlaston had been put to a series of uses by Wedgwood (and had been leased to the Bank of England during the Second World War), but in the 1950s it developed dry rot and become an embarrassment to the company. The building was boarded up and effectively left to decay.

In 1975, SAVE was involved in an inquiry into the first application to demolish. By the time of the second inquiry the house had effectively been abandoned for nearly twenty years and was suffering from extensive coal mining subsidence; and it was likely to suffer still more in the future. The problem was that Barlaston sat above one of the richest coal mines in Europe and the whole village was expected to sink forty feet over the next twenty years. Thanks to the sophistication of modern mining techniques, little damage would have been caused to most other properties.

SAVE ACTION GUIDE

Barlaston's problem was that it sat astride a geological fault (i.e. the junction of two different types of substrata). As a result, settlement was likely to be uneven, and the whole building could tilt as a gap opened up beneath it, breaking its back.

With the help of Kit Martin, the architect Bob Weighton and the engineers Peter Dann and Partners, SAVE presented a scheme at the public inquiry to show that the building could be stabilized and converted on a commercial basis into seven flats. The presentation at the inquiry was masterminded by our solicitor David Cooper aided by Sophie Andreae, then our Secretary. It proved so effective that Wedgwood's QC suddenly threw down the gauntlet to those he had continually derided as the 'united aesthetes' saying, 'If you are so sure you can save this building, buy it yourselves for £1.' SAVE accepted the challenge and within hours the inquiry was over, the inspector having gallantly offered the 10p deposit.

SAVE was now the owner of a building we had not so far gained access to. The first sight was daunting. All the floorboards had been removed, and the ceilings and plasterwork had crashed down into the

Barlaston Hall, Staffordshire. One of SAVE's best known campaigns led to its purchase for £1. Since then funds have been raised to finance restoration

COUNTRY HOUSES

basement with the weight of water pouring through the roof. The main staircase had collapsed long ago; only the upper flight remained, hanging precariously in space. The back staircase collapsed a few weeks later. But in a strange way the desperate state of the house opened up its history and construction to our eyes: in an eighteenth-century building everything is usually concealed behind plasterwork. But here we could see for ourselves how timber-framed partition walls, filled in with brickwork, were used on the upper storeys over the larger rooms to ensure no weight pressed on their ceilings; and how joiners had constructed the mahogany bookcases in the library. And because Barlaston had ceased to function as a house in the 1930s, and had not been modernized for many years before that, it was in a remarkably unaltered state and thus an important archaeological document.

Our first step was to set up an independent trust to repair the building. The immediate task was then to get a secure temporary roof across the whole building so that the interior could begin to dry out in the spring. The trust at this stage had not one penny to its name but the Historic Buildings Council came forward with a ninety per cent grant for emergency works.

Over the next four years, with the help of further Historic Building Council grants and the support of the Manifold Trust, the whole of the external structure was successfully restored: the house was given a permanent roof; the brickwork was repaired and the numerous cracks stitched up; and all the remarkable octagonal window sashes repaired or replaced. All this work was done by Swan and Partners, a small building company whose partners took the closest possible interest in the work, with Sophie Andreae making a weekly pilgrimage to supervise the job.

Meanwhile, very serious problems had developed with the National Coal Board. At the inquiry they had stated that, if the Secretary of State decided the house should be preserved, they would pay not only for past subsidence damage but also for preventative works, in the form of a raft underneath the building, which could be jacked up to correct the effect of any subsidence.

Now, however, the Coal Board took the view that as the Secretary of State had never formally ruled on the consent to demolish following the inquiry, they were not obliged to honour their undertaking. Instead we were directed to a clause in the Coal Act which enabled the Coal Board to offer minimal compensation for a building in a very derelict state.

Michael Heseltine, as Secretary of State for the Environment, had taken a strong line on Barlaston, using his powers to carry out emergency repairs for the first time. His successors were less committed and procrastinated interminably. All this time, SAVE was being advised by Robert Carnwath. The problem was that the provisions of the Coal Act had never been tested in court. In previous cases the Coal Board had either paid up or the owner had agreed to demolition. According to the Act, three conditions had to be met if the Board was to pay for the repair and stabilization of the building. The Secretary of State had first to rule that the building was of outstanding architectural interest, which Michael Heseltine had done. In addition, he had to certify that restoration was both practicable and in the public interest.

These last two assurances, his successors had inexplicably failed to provide. The future of Barlaston now looked desperate. Robert Carnwath feared that the Act was so confused that we could not go to court with a realistic chance of winning. Sensing this, the Coal Board struck what was intended to be a mortal blow—refusing to carry out the preventative works and offering us a mere £25,000 towards past damage which had been estimated at well over £100,000.

This was so demonstrably unfair that SAVE was able to hit back by seeking leave for judicial review. The writ named the Secretary of State for the Environment as the first party for failing to provide the necessary certificates, with the Coal Board conjoined as second party. Happily, the Department of the Environment was so appalled at being cast as the number one villain that the certificates came almost by return of post and the Coal Board now felt isolated and exposed. They agreed to come to the negotiating table and Robert Carnwath, with their counsel, drafted terms of agreement under which a settlement could be worked out.

Eventually, the Coal Board, by now reconstituted as British Coal, agreed to pay some £120,000 in compensation, as well as our legal fees, and to fund preventative works.

One of the conditions of the original purchase from Wedgwood was that it could buy back the house for £1 if we had not completed the restoration within five years. The expiry date loomed as we prepared to go to court, but to our relief Wedgwood agreed a three-year extension in recognition of the work we had done. By the time the complex details of the preventative works had been finally drawn up and agreed we were again running out of time. Now Wedgwood generously agreed to waive the buy-back clause in return for a series of covenants ensuring that the house would be restored and looked after in the future.

Now that the preventative works are almost complete, the trust has been able, with the help of a grant from English Heritage and a loan from the National Heritage Memorial Fund to put back the floors. For the first time in years it is possible to walk around the whole building and experience it in three dimensions. Presently, we are looking to the completion of the scheme, either as flats or possibly as a small hotel or restaurant.

Barlaston could be described as the Gettysburg or even the Stalingrad battle for preservation in England, the place where against overwhelming and continuous odds an outstanding building has been preserved and revived. No major country house has faced a greater catalogue of danger and decay than Barlaston, with the combined problems of twenty years of rain cascading through the roof and repeated bouts of coal mining subsidence. If Barlaston can be saved, no other major country house need be forsaken.

② COUNTRY HOUSE PARKS

'PARKS THERE ARE in England more than in all Europe.' So wrote Peter Heylen in his *Cosmographie* of 1677. Although the English landscape park is often thought of as a creation of the eighteenth century, by William Kent, Capability Brown and Humphry Repton, many country house parks are much older in origin, and in numerous instances are marked on Elizabethan county maps.

The essence of a country house park is that it is a large area of grazing, uninterrupted by hedges or fences, in which animals are free to roam at will. The illusion is of savannah-like country scattered with trees in an apparently natural state. Many parks were deer parks, others were grazed by cattle, sheep and horses.

Unfortunately, the overwhelming majority of surviving herds of deer either died off or escaped when country houses were requisitioned during the Second World War; the 'Dig for Victory' campaign meant that much ancient pasture was ploughed and used as arable land which was often never reseeded.

In the years after the war, with the drive for ever-increasing agricultural productivity, country house parks were often seen as areas of 'conspicuous waste', which could be better put to more intensive cultivation. This ignored the fact that many had been created out of poor arable land or even poorer scrub. The great park at Petworth was described by Arthur Young in 1793 as previously consisting only of 'bushes, furze, some timber and rubbish of no kind of use'.

Despite ploughing, despite the ravages of age and elm disease on park trees, the essential features of parks often survive—namely, the encircling shelter belts and individual clumps of trees, and the lakes. As has been made clear in the discussion of country houses, parks and the houses that stand within them are inseparable. The prospect of a house secure in beautiful parkland will be better than one where the approach is ploughed right up to the ha-ha.

SAVE ACTION GUIDE

Country house parkland, however, deserves to be recognized and protected as an artistic creation in its own right. 'What were known all over the world as "English gardens" were the most pervasive influence that England ever had on the European way of life', wrote Lord Clark. Repton made the same point in his *Sketches and Hints* of 1794: 'To improve the scenery of country and to display its native beauties with advantage is an art which originated in England.'

There is at present no effective form of protection for landscape parks. Designation as a conservation area and inclusion in the English Heritage Register of Parks and Gardens are important first steps, but they are not enough.

Most county record offices will have estate plans showing parks in the eighteenth and early nineteenth centuries in considerable detail. The early versions of Ordnance Survey maps are also very useful—particularly the large-scale, six inch to one mile maps. These show individual trees.

The aerial photographic units of both Aerofilms and Cambridge University have extensive coverage of country house gardens and parks. In addition, there will usually be descriptions of notable parks in early topographical works, particularly *Views of Gentlemen's Seats*, as well as county histories, local guides and even the standard White's County Gazeteers.

From these sources, it is possible quite quickly to gain an idea of how parkland has changed over the years—usually expanding in the later eighteenth and early nineteenth centuries, and then contracting during the twentieth.

Threats to parks come first of all from road building and secondly from increasing leisure development, notably golf courses.

With road proposals, it is vital to object as strongly as possible at the earliest opportunity, even if you are told no route has yet been chosen. The Department of Transport, in particular, tends to have a preferred route from a very early date, and then to stick to it. Make the case for the park in historical and aesthetic terms as strongly, publicly and early as you can. If possible, engage the advice of a civil engineer experienced in road building. English Heritage will advise on this. Very often it will be possible to put forward an alternative or modified route, and sometimes, for an inquiry, the Department may undertake to draw this up in detail.

The threat from golf comes both from the change in the character of pasture and from associated development. A golf course is only rarely a paying proposition in itself: the real gain in value comes from obtaining planning permission to build in open countryside.

While there is undoubtedly a demand for more golf courses, it needs to be underlined that many applications are purely speculative. When permission is granted, the owner does not always immediately begin work on a popular local leisure facility, but simply puts the land up for sale at a much higher price.

COUNTRY HOUSE PARKS

Parks, moreover, can provide significant leisure facilities—and revenue—in their own right. A good example is Gunton Park in Norfolk, where the fishing is let by the day, attracting 4,000 or more anglers a year. The eighteenth-century sawmill on the lower lake is being restored by the Norfolk Windmill Trust and will be fully open when restoration is complete. Parks provide space for a whole range of events, from steam rallies to horse shows.

The character of most parks depends substantially on a scattering of trees—whether individually or in clumps. As animals have traditionally been allowed to graze amongst them, the lower branches have been rubbed or eaten away. The trees therefore have the characteristic that you can see under them—the underneath of an oak is almost perfectly level. When grazing ceases the shape of the tree emerges.

The overriding need is to ensure these park trees are not merely protected but replanted. Grants from both the Countryside Commission and English Heritage are sometimes available for this. When parks are ploughed, there is a tendency for farmers to plough closer and closer to the trunk until eventually the tractor disturbs the roots and the tree suffers, or even dies.

With the new set-aside agricultural policies, there is a possibility that cultivated parks can be put back to pasture. Set-aside payments will not be given for parks used for cattle or sheep, but the rules encourage use as deer parks. And what better solution can there be for a decayed or threatened landscape park than for it to become a deer park once again?

Uffington Park, Lincolnshire. Although the house was burned down, the park survives. A golf course development threatened the landscape but plans have been withdrawn for now

SAVE ACTION GUIDE

Case History

HIGHCLERE PARK, HAMPSHIRE

SAVE FIRST WENT to court to protect the magnificent park at Highclere in Hampshire. Here we faced a familiar dilemma: the Department of Transport and the county council were seeking to improve a trunk road and, seeing a large area of parkland, decided to take the new road through the park, cutting off a large swathe near the main entrance gates.

Again and again, SAVE has found the Department of Transport has failed to recognize the value, in historic and aesthetic terms, of country house parkland. Parks are seen simply as a soft option, usually with only one resident to protest, and only one owner to negotiate with, when compulsory purchase proceedings are commenced. The problem is often the more awkward because owners of country houses are hesitant to protest when they realize that other options may bring the new road much closer to the houses of neighbours.

SAVE began by writing to the Department of Transport setting out the importance of the park, only to be told that a large number of representations had been made in favour of the proposed route. We sought to find out what these were so that we could consider the points raised and respond to them. The Department refused to let us see the representations. Following a prolonged correspondence, SAVE issued a writ which came to court. The judge came down forcefully in our favour. 'A properly directed minister acting reasonably could not have been satisfied that a public inquiry was unnecessary in the present case, where two substantial groups with conflicting views were involved', he held. The Secretary of State thus had a duty to call a public inquiry.

The inquiry was duly held in 1984 and here SAVE joined with the Garden History Society to put forward an alternative route prepared by David Jacques.

At the inquiry SAVE faced the opposition not only of the Department of Transport, but also of the county council. The officially preferred route cut across the entrance to the park on an embankment. Although it was proposed to shield this with 'massive planting', this in itself we felt would be a major intrusion. The Department of Transport argued that this was a remote part of the park, far from the house. SAVE's contention was that the entrance to a park was of crucial importance, however distant it was from the house itself. Very careful consideration was given to the layout of drives to provide the best possible views across the parkland. Repton, in his *Hints on Landscape Gardening*, recommends that entrance gates should be placed on the axis of an approaching public road, with a public road curving away to the side, around the park. The inspector accepted our case and the new road has been constructed following our proposals.

③ GARDENS

GARDEN CONSERVATION IS a relatively new phenomenon. Of course, gardens have long been maintained in conjunction with historic houses; what is new is the desire to rescue and restore gardens that may have been abandoned many years ago, as attractions in their own right. An additional incentive is that a garden, in contrast to its associated historic building, does not always need substantial sums for major fabric repairs at the outset and can be revived over a longer period of time.

With country house gardens, it is important to remember that the grounds consist not only of the lawns and terraces immediately round the house, but also large walled gardens and extensive woodland walks and shrubberies. These wild-looking areas, often planted with fine conifers, were especially popular in the nineteenth century; but wilderness gardens, informally laid out, also date from the eighteenth century, and even earlier—Henry VIII's palace at Nonsuch in Surrey had one.

But of course, not all early gardens resemble parkland. Recent research, aided by aerial photography, has revealed traces of sixteenth- and seventeenth-century formal gardens of a type that was thought to have been entirely destroyed during the naturalistic craze of the eighteenth century.

With such ancient remains, the first need is to accord them the same protection as other ancient monuments. With more recent gardens, there are exciting possibilities of restoring them to their original appearance.

The remarkable Victorian garden at Biddulph in Staffordshire, created by the orchid-loving James Bateman, was laid out as a series of continents and countries—Egypt with a temple in clipped yew and China hidden away behind great rocks.

The gardens had been reasonably well maintained by a hospital but, as closure and sale loomed, their future became increasingly uncertain. What counts in cases such as this is ensuring continued pressure and publicity at national level, while also working with a local group, which can keep up

SAVE ACTION GUIDE

Biddulph Grange, Staffordshire. One of the oriental features of this very special Victorian garden which is now owned by the National Trust

pressure on the spot by stirring up the interest of local authorities and the regional branch of the National Trust.

Part of the problem at Biddulph was that the hospital service was being reorganized, and the outgoing authority would not bind the hands of its successor by making a decision. Steady pressure, however, persuaded the National Heritage Memorial Fund to provide the endowment needed for the National Trust to take it on.

At The Moot, Downton, a remarkable garden has been rescued by a preservation trust set up by local people. This is a very special but long-abandoned eighteenth-century garden, laid out on the remains of a medieval motte and bailey castle. It stood across the public road, separated from its pretty, early eighteenth-century house; in addition to this geographical separation, house and garden each had a different owner. A trust has now been able to acquire it and take the first steps towards long-term restoration.

Case History
HACKFALL, NORTH YORKSHIRE

THE SAVIOUR OF Hackfall took the unexpected form of the Woodland Trust. Hackfall was created in the mid-eighteenth century by William Aislabie, the owner of Studley Royal, the beautiful baroque water garden next to Fountains Abbey. Whereas the gardens at Studley Royal are formal and geometric, Hackfall is rugged, picturesque and romantic.

GARDENS

But for years the garden, with its extraordinary follies and temples, had been decaying, and it was clear that soon no more than a few heaps of stone would be left. All the good timber had been felled and sold in the 1930s and saplings had quickly crowded out the original vistas.

Our publicity drew attention to Hackfall's plight. Like many other historic properties, Hackfall belonged to an owner who reputedly would never sell. The softly, softly approach had been tried, but to no avail. There are few substitutes for a firm, measured article in the national press, drawing attention to the historical interest of a threatened place. Even if an owner's first reaction is hostile, quite soon after action may be forthcoming. Following an article in the *Sunday Telegraph*, the owner of Hackfall decided to sell.

A local trust has now been set up to champion the restoration of the landscape; and the Landmark Trust has taken on the principal building, the splendid banqueting house, constructed with three great arches, overlooking the valley like one of the fountains of baroque Rome.

A difficult problem arises with gardens in towns and cities. Pressure on land may be very strong, making it impossible to raise funds to even acquire the garden, let alone restore it. The situation here is the more acute as historic town gardens retaining important features are very rare in Britain. And while many Victorian villas and large, early twentieth-century suburban houses have, or did have, extensive gardens with fountains and

Hackfall, North Yorkshire. A local trust is now raising funds to restore the gardens and buildings, neglected for many years

follies, they have been surprisingly little studied. Many are completely unknown.

One such was a remarkable grotto-garden built for a South African diamond mining millionaire at Merrow Grange on the outskirts of Guildford, in Surrey. This stood overgrown and decaying in the grounds of a convent school. The convent wanted to sell part of the grounds for development; the local council was sympathetic while being the first to recognize the importance of the garden. In the end, the compromise was to give permission for the new blocks of apartments, but to require that the remains of the grottoes be restored as a feature in the new development.

Houses with large grounds in the outskirts of historic towns or major cities attract infill development. A property company may promise restoration of the house in return for permission to build in the grounds.

In some cases, infill development of this kind may be irresistible, but it is important that the quality and potential of the garden should be assessed first. Also, while large private grounds in towns may seem an anachronism, they often provide important 'green lungs', and their lofty trees and lawns provide an amenity to any passer-by.

In view of the scarcity of historic town gardens, it is worth drawing attention to the precedent of the garden of the Paca House in Annapolis, capital of Maryland, USA. The 1770s house had become a boarding house and the eighteenth-century garden paved over as the city bus station. A dedicated group of local people determined to reconstruct the garden and were able to acquire the whole property when the bus station moved. Using the evidence of extensive archaeology, a remarkable and beautiful garden has been created. Interestingly, it is now so much in demand for weddings, conferences, company launches and events that it easily pays its way. Gardens can be thriving, living things in more ways than one.

Just one of Hackfall's buildings needing restoration

④ GARDEN BUILDINGS, FOLLIES AND TEMPLES

GARDEN BUILDINGS, FOR all their obvious fascination, can pose severe problems. How can owners, often already hard-pressed to maintain their houses, be expected to find further sums for buildings that are purely ornamental?

Fortunately, the Historic Buildings Councils, from their inception in 1953, recognized the special problems and significance of garden buildings and have often offered a higher than normal proportion of grant aid to secure their restoration. However, significant numbers of remarkable follies remain isolated, abandoned or decaying, and in 1987 SAVE published a catalogue, *Pavilions in Peril*, illustrating forty examples.

The situation is not as hopeless as it might seem. The Landmark Trust has rescued dozens of follies and temples from decay, ranging from the Swiss Cottage at Endsleigh in Devon, to the Pineapple at Dunmore near Stirling, in Scotland.

The Landmark Trust restores its buildings for holiday letting, rented for a week or fortnight at a time in summer, but sometimes for weekends in winter. Holiday letting is unquestionably the best solution in many cases. Were these buildings to become permanent homes, they would soon sprout extensions and garages and be surrounded by lawns and flower-beds, which would change their rustic character.

The Landmark Trust is always willing to consider new candidates for restoration and is often restoring up to a dozen buildings at any one time.

Some follies, however, do not provide suitable accommodation or are simply too small. They need help of a different kind. Ten years ago, SAVE floated the idea of a new society, the Friends of Friendless Garden Buildings. Nothing happened until, quite independently, a group of enthusiasts set up the Folly Fellowship in 1988. Their main focus of activity is an excellent, simply produced newsletter. Such is the delight that people take in seeking out follies at weekends that the Fellowship has quickly gathered momentum.

SAVE ACTION GUIDE

The Chateau at Gate Burton, Lincolnshire. Before, **above**, *and after,* **below**, *restoration by the Landmark Trust*

GARDEN BUILDINGS, FOLLIES AND TEMPLES

Another enterprising venture of this kind is the Ice House Hunt, dedicated to identifying and mapping all surviving ice houses. Virtually every substantial country house had an ice house and it is surprising how many remain.

Other follies will be found in groups, built as part of a wild garden some distance from the house. Examples are the rugged stone seats in the woods above Jervaulx Abbey in North Yorkshire or the temples at Halswell House in Somerset. With patience, it may be possible to track down not only buildings and the foundations of lost buildings, but also grottoes, seats, cascades and artificial rockwork.

At Wentworth Woodhouse in Yorkshire the remarkable follies are now vested in the Fitzwilliam Amenity Trust which has restored the spectacular mausoleum built by John Carr and opened it to the public.

With small, isolated follies and temples, one solution is to let them out to artists. The Fishing Temple at Sharpham in Devon has been let in this way for many years. Charitable trusts, regional arts associations and individual patrons might be willing to sponsor a pilot scheme on these lines.

As garden buildings were often architecturally ambitious and elaborately decorated, great care is needed to use the correct materials and finishes when restoring them. Where a temple, folly or grotto has been long abandoned and the roof has collapsed, bringing down the ceiling with it, a careful archaeological sift must be made through the debris. It may throw up pieces of plasterwork,shellwork and panelling, fragments of windows and evidence of colour schemes.

Case History
HAMPTON COURT HOUSE, SURREY

ONE OF THE best rescues involving archaeological research was that of the grotto at Hampton Court House in the garden of Lord Halifax's house, opposite Wolsey's palace. Interest in the grotto and gardens was stirred by SAVE and in particular by an article Eileen Harris wrote for *Country Life*. The London Borough of Richmond, which ran the house as a home for the elderly, raised funds for an exemplary restoration programme. The complex decoration was restored with masterly skill by the sculptor Simon Verity.

Attention must also be paid to the landscape setting of follies. Many were built as focal points of vistas that have since been obscured by trees; others stood in the centre of a grove of trees. While temples built in the later eighteenth century may have stood in a naturalistic landscape inspired by the paintings of Claude, earlier garden buildings almost certainly stood in more formal settings, and fragments of avenues or long overgrown yew and beech hedges may remain.

SAVE ACTION GUIDE

Precisely because garden buildings are so appealing, local authorities have sometimes undertaken their restoration: a good example is the grotto at Ware, restored by the district council.

Eighteenth-century maps of historic towns often show elaborate formal gardens behind the houses, but very few traces of these remain. The one feature that does survive in various historic towns is the Georgian summer house, often square with a pyramid roof and perched on a corner above a garden wall to take advantage of the view. A remarkable series survives in Kendal in Cumbria.

More study needs to be made of garden buildings and structures in later Victorian and Edwardian town gardens, which were often laid out on an elaborate scale and contain interesting features that have been entirely forgotten; these are in danger of destruction as the gardens of suburban houses are divided up for redevelopment.

⑤ BARNS AND OTHER FARM BUILDINGS

THE ANCIENT BARNS, cow sheds, granaries and other agricultural buildings of the countryside are a vital if perhaps under-appreciated part of Britain's architectural heritage. There is certainly nothing new in converting farm buildings. Since the building of the huge medieval tithe barns, constant changes in farming methods have meant that most farm buildings have had to be adapted to new uses or else demolished or simply abandoned to the elements. It is during the latter part of this century, however, that historic barns and other traditional rural buildings have faced their greatest threat.

By 1987, there were more applications to demolish listed barns than any other single building type. On the other hand, the massive increase in conversions of redundant barns to homes had led to calls to halt entirely the conversion of historic barns into houses. To highlight the problem, and to try to explore solutions, SAVE published a report, *A Future for Farm Buildings*, which illustrated the many uses to which farm buildings could be put without compromising their character or integrity.

Farm buildings vary enormously in type, layout and character, from one part of the country to another. A large timber barn in Essex, standing isolated near a road, will undoubtedly suffer if it is suddenly surrounded by the trimmings of a suburban garden—tarmac drive, garage, lawns, flowerbeds, hedges and off-the-peg fences. Elsewhere in the country, there are groups of farm buildings laid out on a courtyard plan that can undergo a complete change of use with virtually no visible alterations to the external appearance.

In all such cases, there are a number of important guidelines. Principally, the landscaping must be in keeping with the area: gravel is better than tarmac, and interesting features must be retained.

Not all barns are in open countryside. Many ancient villages contain venerable barns built of the same materials as local cottages. In some areas, the farms were actually congregated in the villages, and behind the farmhouses on the streets there may be barns of considerable length. These may be suitable for converting into one or more cottages.

Much has been made of the possibilities of converting barns for light industrial use. Clearly such use has its attractions: it is quite similar to the original use, and it may provide local employment. Barns are best suited to operations of a 'craft' nature, rather than larger industrial undertakings. But even a craft workshop can require car-parks, loading bays and improved access, all of which can change the character of the place as much as a residential conversion. The key must be to utilize a group of barns, cow sheds or other such buildings laid out round a farmyard, so that vehicles can be parked out of sight.

New uses may generate traffic—particularly heavy traffic which may not be welcomed by local residents. And, as any successful enterprise will expand, there may soon be pressure to extend the premises, damaging the character of the place in the process. On the other hand, if the industrial use generates low profits, there may not be enough money to maintain the building.

With barns, as well as churches, the good uses need to be measured in terms of their impact on interiors as well as exteriors. The best feature of many barns is the superb carpentry of the timber roof. This may actually be seen to better advantage in conversion to offices or even a house.

In such schemes, it is important to preserve, as far as possible, the openness of the interior—the sense of length and the view into the roof. If enclosed rooms have to be created, this may be better done—in the case of a house—by putting bedrooms and bathrooms on the ground floor or in a 'stack' at one end. If the main living space is at first-floor level, the roof can be left open to create a large, studio-type space.

Now that so many people work at computer terminals, the need for natural light in offices has, against all expectations, decreased. An office conversion of a barn might be the best way to avoid having to introduce unsightly new windows.

Large new windows have undoubtedly been the ruin of many barns, introducing voids where solid facades dominated, producing shiny surfaces amidst matt, weathered ones. One solution is to set the glass back as much as a foot and to use thick, matured timber mullions to break up the surface.

Upland valleys present additional problems because of their often numerous isolated field barns—sometimes one for each hay meadow. Valleys in the Yorkshire Dales are scattered with dozens of these field barns, virtually all disused. Their impact lies in their sheer number: preserving just a few would mean accepting the loss in character of a remarkable and memorable landscape.

A few years ago, the problem seemed insuperable, but now the National Parks Authority, the Countryside Commission and English Heritage have launched a pilot programme. This offers a very high level (up to eighty per

BARNS AND OTHER FARM BUILDINGS

The Moat House, Fisher's Pond, Hampshire. A sensitive conversion of a historic barn to a private home

cent) of grant aid to repair those field barns in Swaledale that remain unconverted. At Chatsworth, in the Peak District, and in the National Parks, isolated barns are also being adapted as simple refuges or camping accommodation. Used in such a way, there is no requirement for electricity, telephones, mains water or drainage.

Case History
TITHE BARN, PILTON, SOMERSET

DEVELOPERS OFTEN TRY to wear down local opposition by continually resubmitting plans. If a new application is submitted, even with very minor alterations, the applicant can claim that previous objections are not relevant. Everyone must therefore renew their objections, amending them as appropriate. Persistence is everything.

In the Somerset village of Pilton, a developer purchased thirteen acres of orchards and woodland including the magnificent grade I listed tithe barn which, despite having lost its roof in a fire, survived as proud as many medieval castles and abbeys. Proposals were put forward for new houses and development around the barn; but because the barn itself was ignored, there were fears for its future. SAVE objected to the scheme and cited examples where tithe barns, 'the cathedrals of farm architecture', had been vested with the National Trust or other preservation trusts. As a consequence, the scheme was withdrawn.

SAVE ACTION GUIDE

Case History

THE STABLES AT CAPEL MANOR, ENFIELD, NORTH LONDON

SO MANY OLD buildings have become redundant that there is a special interest now in any where the original use has prevailed. One of SAVE's more curious cases is the stables at Capel Manor, Enfield, North London. These were leased to HAPPA (Horses and Ponies Protection Association), which was particularly proud of the buildings and wished them to remain. The owners, Enfield Borough Council, wanted to reclaim the stables for use as a canteen by the college in the main house. On a visit, we discovered that all the original stable fittings—the mahogany loose box partitions, wavy railings and brass finials—were still intact. We persuaded the Secretary of State that this was an application important enough for him to determine, and we await the outcome.

Enfield Gazette, 19 July 1990. Reports on the stables at Capel Manor which have been listed following a request by SAVE

⑥ CHURCHES

CHURCHES AND CHAPELS continue to form a major part of the work of SAVE, particularly the serious problem of what can be done when they become redundant and are closed.

Change and Decay

1977 saw the opening of the major Victoria and Albert Museum exhibition, 'Change and Decay: The Future of our Churches', which was organized by two of SAVE's committee members. The major aim of this exhibition was to provide the ammunition to persuade the Government that historic building grants must be introduced for historic churches. Until then, because of the Ecclesiastical Exemption, which exempts churches in use from listed building controls, grants had been limited to secular buildings on the principle 'no control: no money'.

However, it was evident that if the deadlock were not broken soon, ever greater numbers of very fine churches would be closed and demolished. Exactly a month after the exhibition opened, the Secretary of State announced that state aid for churches in use would begin with immediate effect at the rate of £1 million a year.

A large travelling version of the exhibition was later prepared by SAVE, and shown in major museums and galleries all round the country over a period of three years. This provoked the Church Commissioners to mount their own exhibition to counter some of the criticism voiced in the SAVE exhibition, and this was sent on a tour of cathedrals.

The V & A exhibition made a strong attack on the number of churches that the Church Commissioners had agreed to demolish immediately as being redundant and of only marginal architectural interest, without making any effort to find a new use for them.

To this, the Church Commissioners ostensibly had a good answer: that the percentage of listed churches demolished was actually lower than that of secular buildings.

Demolished churches

Left *Holy Trinity, Rugby;* **above left** *Unitarian Chapel, Northgate, Halifax;* **above right** *Holy Trinity, Birkenhead;* **centre left** *All Saints, Brightside, Sheffield;* **centre right** *Cemetery Chapel, Amesbury;* **below** *St Stephen's, Newcastle upon Tyne*

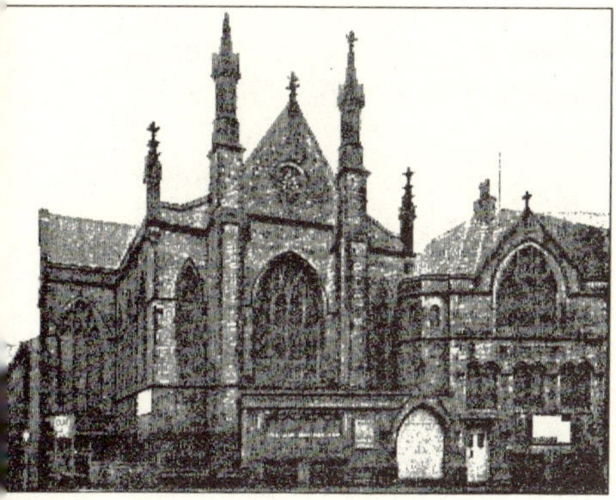

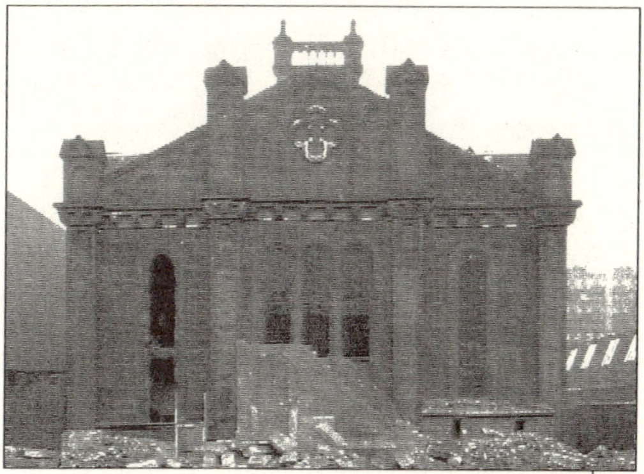

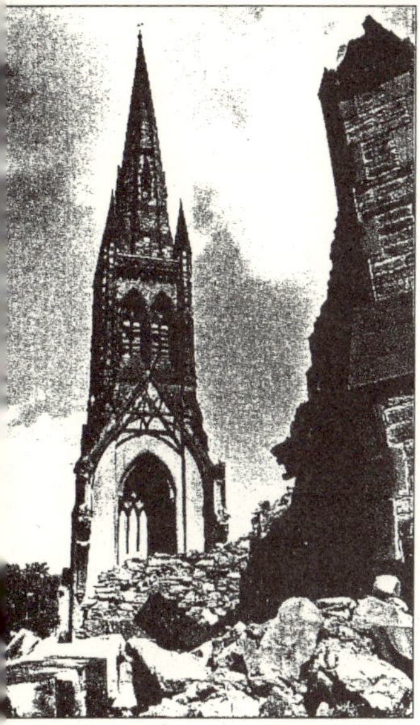

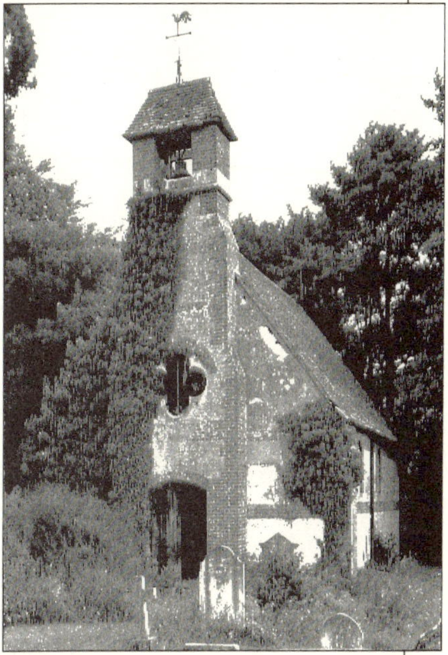

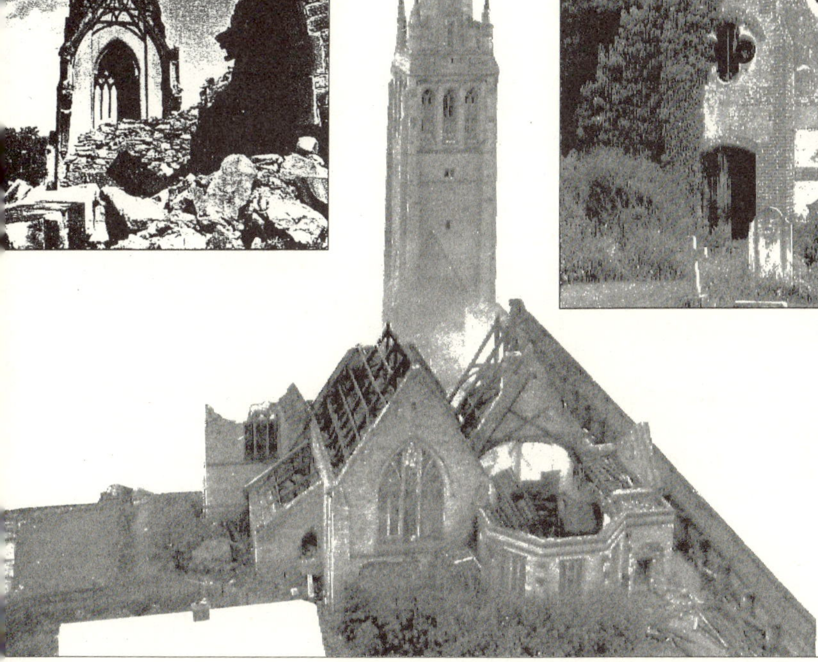

However, this concealed the fact that many 'listable' churches had never actually been listed, for, as the Church was exempt from listed building control, no systematic attempt had been made to list any but the most obvious churches.

Research showed that the main areas of redundancy were in the inner cities and the remote countryside. Many of these churches were included in SAVE's report, *Churches at Risk*.

The exhibition also aimed to show the whole range of suitable alternative uses to which churches could be put—as theatres, concert halls, museums, arts and community centres, and libraries. This was expanded upon in a SAVE book ten years later, *Churches: A Question of Conversion*, which received wide acclaim and is much used by church authorities, planners, parishioners and architects.

It is encouraging to note that, since 1977, not only have many more churches been listed, but a serious effort has also been made to find new uses for a much higher percentage of redundant churches—although procedures remain unnecessarily complicated and frustrating.

Case History
CHURCH OF ST MARK, NORTH AUDLEY STREET, LONDON

THIS RICH VICTORIAN church, in the heart of Mayfair, has lain empty and unused since 1974. St Mark's was at one time one of the most popular and best-attended churches, when Mayfair was truly a residential area. For some years, it was used by the American Church, which offered to buy it for a substantial sum from the London diocese when its lease expired; but the offer was refused and the church declared redundant.

St Mark's is of particular architectural interest, being a Regency church of 1825 with a spectacular and highly ornate Victorian interior by Blomfield, dating from the 1870s. Subsequently, St Mark's has received many enrichments in the form of stained glass, memorials and other fittings. It is listed grade I.

Failing continued worship by the Americans, St Mark's should have been vested in the Redundant Churches Fund once it was closed. But the diocese, seeking to realize maximum financial gain for the valuable site, has pursued a series of schemes for wholly unsuitable uses. Meanwhile, the fabric of the church has suffered greatly, and it now needs large sums for repair.

One of the worst proposals put forward for the church was to turn it into a hamburger joint, run by the restaurant chain, Garfunkels: hardly a use compatible with the dignity of a historic church. The chancel would be used for a bar, the pulpit and font used as containers for plants, and the

CHURCHES

nave filled with fixed 'banquette' seating in booths. SAVE's report, *From Holiness to Hamburgers*, was produced to fight these plans at a public inquiry and the scheme was rejected.

Several years later, the future of this great church is still uncertain. Plans for conversion into a banking hall and offices are probably the most acceptable so far in that they would involve minimal disruption to the interior and would generate the large sums needed to repair the building fully. But there is still controversy over whether this is too much of a compromise, and the church continues to deteriorate.

This stalemate situation is a familiar one to SAVE. Owners of a historic building on a valuable site who are determined to realize substantial sums on the property often allow the building to decay during the years of indecision.

Redundancy

The procedures for closing and disposing of redundant Anglican churches are long and cumbersome.

Policies on redundancy vary sharply from diocese to diocese. Some, like Salisbury, have made dozens of churches redundant. By contrast, the Diocese of Truro has closed very few.

Some churches are closed against the will of local people to fit in with diocesan pastoral plans. One problem is that once closure is mooted congregations may melt away, services may become less frequent and the will to continue is eroded. Where there is strong local determination to keep the church open, the diocese may change its mind and ultimately the Church Commissioners may overrule the plans for closure.

If there is a whisper of redundancy, do not be deflected by talk that it is all in the very early stages, too soon for public discussion, and by promises that there will be plenty of opportunities for comment and debate at an appropriate stage later on. Take action now.

It is important to contact the Council for the Care of Churches, 83 London Wall, London EC2M 5NA. It will be asked in any event to make a detailed assessment of the church's quality and, where two churches are being considered for redundancy, it is likely to make a strong case that the finer and more historic church should continue in use.

Knowledge that there is strong local support for its continuation and use for worship can only help this cause and counter any arguments being put for the other side.

Once again, get in touch with SAVE and other societies, and in particular the local county churches trust—if one exists. The county trusts are almost all dedicated to helping keep churches with small congregations in use for worship and will have good contacts in the diocese. Their addresses can be obtained from the Historic Churches Preservation Trust, Fulham Palace, Bishop's Park, London SW6 6EA.

SAVE ACTION GUIDE

One reason for closure can be a sudden, unexpected bill for repairs. Over £7.1 million is available, however, in grants for churches from English Heritage (with proportionate sums in Scotland and Wales), as well as smaller grants from the Historic Churches Preservation Trust and the county trusts.

A church that is declared redundant enters the so-called 'Waiting Period'. If it is of exceptional quality, there is a chance that it may be vested—either immediately or at a later date—in the Redundant Churches Fund. Clearly, the sooner it is vested the better, as the fund will take over responsibility for maintenance on a regular basis. If you think the church you are concerned about is 'Fund-worthy', find out what the Council for the Care of Churches and the national societies feel about its quality and do all the lobbying you can.

Recommendation for vesting in the Fund, and for appropriate alternative uses, is made by the Advisory Board for Redundant Churches. The ultimate decision, however is taken by the Church Commissioners' own Redundant Churches Committee.

Case History
CHURCH OF ST JOHN THE BAPTIST, AVON DASSETT, WARWICKSHIRE

AT THE END of this pretty Warwickshire village, in a steeply sloping ancient graveyard, stands the Church of St John the Baptist. The finest work of the Victorian architect C. E. Buckeridge, the church's picturesque medieval appearance reflects the earlier church it replaced in 1868.

The church became redundant in 1983, and was closed up and barely maintained. In fact, even the most basic repairs had been neglected for many years before that, so that structural problems developed where they might have been avoided. When a pastoral scheme for its demolition was issued, SAVE immediately objected, recommending that it should be vested with the Redundant Churches Fund. The church was an obvious candidate: of outstanding architectural quality, a vital part of a village conservation area and, with its problems of location and car-parking, not easily adaptable to new uses. St John the Baptist had to be preserved at all costs.

However, the Church Commissioners disagreed. They wished to proceed with demolition and a public inquiry was held. The Church argued that it was not worth spending such high sums on the building's repair. They said local people would not like to see such a waste of money (even though it would not come from local diocesan funds, whereas the cost of demolition would). We felt this was a particularly provocative stance considering much of the cost could have been saved had action been taken earlier.

CHURCHES

Church of St John the Baptist, Avon Dassett, Warwickshire. Consent for demolition was refused and the church has been vested in the Redundant Churches Fund

As part of their case, the Church made much of the fact that there had been no objection to demolition from within the village. Indeed, they said the small congregation was in favour of demolition as many members were old and infirm and could not climb the steps up to the church. However, with the stories of massive repair costs being bandied around and a particularly uninspiring incumbent devoting most of his energies to the adjacent parish, it was understandable that no-one had been brave enough to voice their concern.

Many people find it hard to counter the argument of 'people before buildings' that the Church puts forward, even though for most of us the visible presence of a church—whether still in religious use or not—is an important and reassuring symbol of faith to all who pass by. By creating the Redundant Churches Fund, the Church of England has ensured the preservation of some of its very finest buildings. The cost of repair is met primarily by the Department of the Environment (seventy per cent), and the remainder is contributed by the Church.

The outcome of the inquiry was a triumphant acceptance of our case and a recommendation that the church go to the Redundant Churches Fund. This the Commissioners accepted, and St John the Baptist remains part of the village scene at Avon Dassett.

Case History
CHURCH OF ALL SOULS, HALIFAX

EVEN BEFORE IT was declared redundant in 1977, All Souls looked a lost cause. Gilbert Scott had said that it was 'on the whole, my finest church', but Colonel Akroyd, who had built it as the centrepiece of his remarkable village of Akroyd, had never sufficiently endowed it. The church was vast, with a tower and spire of cathedral proportions, and far beyond the resources of a small congregation.

An engineer's report had condemned the spire as dangerous and said that it must be dismantled. Once the church lost its dominant feature, the case for saving the church would evaporate altogether.

All Souls was a church of such outstanding quality, with magnificent fittings of every kind, that it was essential to preserve it intact. The Church Commissioners, however, had always been reluctant to vest urban churches in the Redundant Churches Fund and made it absolutely clear that they considered All Souls would impose an impossible burden on the resources of the Fund. Attempts had been made to find alternative uses, but it was evident that nothing suitable was forthcoming.

The likelihood loomed that there would be a major public inquiry, that a Dangerous Structures Notice would be served on the spire, that the spire would then be truncated and the church mutilated, and that rain would start pouring through the roof, resulting in a massive outbreak of dry rot. Even if we were ultimately victorious at a public inquiry, the church would have suffered so grievously during the Waiting Period that a large part of its artistic quality and integrity would have been lost.

SAVE therefore decided the only way forward was to establish a new independent trust to take on the task of urgent major repairs. The sums involved were colossal: over £0.5 million for the spire and the roof.

Thanks to enthusiastic support from Jennifer Jenkins, chairman of the Historic Buildings Council, we were offered a very high level of grant towards the roof. As a result of nail sickness, the heavy Westmorland slates were regularly coming loose and crashing down with such force that they sliced through the lead gutters below. All Souls suffered like many Victorian churches from high, inaccessible valley gutters, which became clogged and allowed damp to seep into the building. Our architect, the appropriately named Donald Buttress, devised an ingenious means of resolving the problem. All Souls was given a new roof oversailing the

CHURCHES

Church of All Souls, Halifax, West Yorkshire. Rescued by SAVE, it is now vested in the Redundant Churches Fund

upper parapets, throwing water directly on to the lower aisle roofs. We could not afford to retile the roof with Westmorland slates, but the sheer urgency of making the church watertight ruled this out anyway.

Donald Buttress' solution was to tile the roof with ridged composition tiles of a greenish grey hue, which from below look remarkably similar to slates and blend very well with the stonework.

The main challenge was the stabilization of the spire. We applied for a grant from the National Heritage Memorial Fund on the basis that its support alone could save the church. There was heated debate, but by the casting vote of the chairman we got our grant. Working with Arups as engineers, Donald Buttress designed an ingenious means of strengthening the spire *in situ*. The problem was that the spire was just a little too tall and too thin for its own good. The diocese's surveyors had said that 100-mph winds could topple it. We waited anxiously as reports came in of 97-mph gales in the Pennines but thankfully the spire remained firm.

The solution was to strengthen the spire from within by inserting a single skin of new brickwork all the way up to the top, and bolting the brick and stone together with stainless steel pins that would be invisible from the ground.

The work progressed well until it was discovered that the original iron braces inserted into the stonework by Scott had rusted very badly and expanded several inches, forcing the stonework upwards. Once the rusted ironwork was removed, the danger was that the tower would topple over. Arups worked out a method of cutting out the rusted iron in very small sections and strengthening it as they went along. Fears that the spire would have to be dismantled after all were allayed.

The All Souls Trust had taken a seven-year lease on the church and virtually the whole of this time was used on repairs to the spire and roof. At this point, the trustees decided that the future of the church would be best secured by vesting it in the Redundant Churches Fund. After some initial hesitation, the Church Commissioners agreed and now the remaining repairs, principally to the stonework, can be carried out on a rolling programme over several years.

Raising funds for a redundant church is extremely difficult, particularly in a town like Halifax, which was suffering from industrial decline and had numerous other major buildings in search of funds. None the less, the trustees were able to raise more than £70,000 towards the repairs of the church, funds that unlocked the crucial support from English Heritage and the National Heritage Memorial Fund.

All Souls shows that in certain circumstances, where a complete impasse looms, the creation of a one-off building preservation trust can be the vehicle by which an outstanding building can be saved.

Had All Souls been lost, the Church authorities would undoubtedly have used it as a precedent for arguing that there were some churches which, however important, were simply too difficult or expensive to save. By setting up a trust for All Souls and carrying out the essential repairs, SAVE has demonstrated that even the most problematic redundant churches in the most difficult locations need not be a lost cause.

Care of redundant churches

During the Waiting Period the church is legally the responsibility of the local Diocesan Board of Finance. The Boards have a duty to keep the church 'in good repair' but, in SAVE's experience, some fail to carry out even the most basic maintenance.

The situation can quickly become desperate. A neglected church is an invitation to vandalism and very soon after that to arson. The list of churches that have been burnt out during the Waiting Period of redundancy is scandalously long.

The first need is to try and ensure that the churchyard is looked after and kept tidy. Volunteers should be able to carry out the minimal work

CHURCHES

involved, though some dioceses seem curiously reluctant to accept offers of help of this kind.

Secondly, each diocese has a Redundant Churches Uses Committee charged with finding new uses or new owners for churches in the Waiting Period. Make contact with the chairman of the Uses Committee and press him to place the church in the hands of the local office of one of the national estate agents. The only cost involved may be that of advertising the property and, even if the diocese is reluctant to do this, it should be persuaded it is worthwhile. In some cases, however, estate agents will do a certain amount of advertising free of charge.

The threat of demolition

Even if the Church Commissioners decide to proceed with demolition, all is not yet lost. Under the redundancy procedures of the Pastoral Measure, authorized by Parliament, listed building consent is not required; but a special procedure has been agreed with the Department of the Environment whereby a public inquiry will be held if the church is listed. This provides a forum for everyone to express their views, challenge the need for demolition and put forward alternatives. Technically, the inquiry is non-statutory and therefore the Church Commissioners are not bound by its recommendations, but the likelihood is that they will abide by them, as in the case of the village church of St John the Baptist in Avon Dassett. This is the moment for local and national societies to put forward schemes for alternative uses in detail and to question whether the church has been marketed in an effective fashion.

Case History
CHURCH OF ST MARY-IN-THE-CASTLE, HASTINGS, SUSSEX

ONE OF THE finest Regency churches in England, St Mary-in-the-Castle is the centrepiece of an impressive and grand crescent of stuccoed houses designed by Joseph Kay in 1824–28. This crescent, with the noble Ionic portico of St Mary's facing directly on to the seafront, is potentially one of the finest architectural set-pieces along the south coast.

St Mary's had a sad and long history of neglect. Closed as a church in 1970, it had passed through several owners, all of whom had had different plans for the building, the final one being to open it as a World War II museum. Meanwhile, the church was suffering dreadfully from damp, dry rot, water penetration and vandalism.

In the autumn of 1986, SAVE received an SOS from a Hastings resident who had read reports that the church was facing possible demolition. The local newspaper published a letter from the Queen Mother, as patron of the Georgian Group, expressing her concern for the building.

Hastings Borough Council had been pursuing compulsory purchase of the building but, in the light of surveyors' reports apparently quoting costs of £2.5 million for repairs alone, made a last-minute decision against this and served a Dangerous Structures Notice instead. This rang alarm bells, for if, as was likely, the owner did not comply with this, the interior of the church, if not the facade, could be demolished for safety reasons.

SAVE's first priority was to persuade the council that such a desperate measure could be avoided. Having always been sceptical of such high figures for repairs being bandied about, we commissioned our own structural survey which, more reassuringly, estimated the cost of urgent repairs to be £250,000. We then took a trip to the seaside on a cold, grey November day to meet the council and other interested bodies.

As a result of the meeting and subsequent publicity, it was resolved that the council would indeed proceed with compulsory purchase, that study would be undertaken to explore new uses for the building and that English Heritage would grant substantial aid for repairs.

It was encouraging to receive a letter from the Hastings Urban Conservation Project a few months later saying, 'The Borough Council are talking in positive terms about the future of the building ... The balance has tipped from viewing the problem entirely in terms of liability and expense to acknowledging that it also offers an opportunity ... There is no doubt that the progress achieved to date has to a significant extent been the result of your backing.'

Unfortunately, there have been a few more hurdles since then. St Mary's, although nearly repaired to satisfactory condition, still needs a new use. The council now owns the church, the house next door and a shop in front but are looking for ideas and offers of ownership. An ideal solution would be a public/private partnership for some sort of arts-related use, as the church offers such a splendid space inside.

Warning! Demolition under faculty

Most churches are demolished under the Pastoral Measure, but a diocese or parish may decide to proceed under faculty. This means they must obtain a faculty from the chancellor of the diocese. In some cases, Church authorities have proceeded in this way because they felt that permission was more likely to be forthcoming.

The key point to bear in mind is that, even if a faculty is granted, listed building consent is also required for demolition. Be sure to alert the local planning authority, which may not be aware of the subtleties of the legislation. In such cases, a local planning committee has full power to reject the application and of course the Secretary of State can call a public inquiry.

The procedures are clearly set out in the planning circulars. Whether a church is to be rebuilt on the same site or the land sold for development, listed building consent must be obtained.

CHURCHES

This provides you with the opportunity to make objections in the same way as with any other listed building and to put forward alternative solutions. The usual test applies: Has the freehold building been offered for sale on the open market?

The respective Secretaries of State have powers to call the matter in to public inquiry. If the local authority decides to grant consent, the Secretary of State has twenty-eight days to consider whether to call in the case and decide for himself. Therefore, be ready to press for an inquiry in such circumstances if you consider there is a fighting chance that the church can be saved.

There are abundant examples of good new uses for churches and many of these have only emerged in the final stages of battles over individual churches.

Warning! Partial demolition

The law on listed churches was established in a classic House of Lords case (Bedfordshire County Council v Howard United Reformed Trustees, 1974). The Trustees had claimed that, as a new place of worship was to be incorporated on the redeveloped site, the Ecclesiastical Exemption applied. However, the Law Lords took the common-sense view that it was ridiculous to say a building was 'for the time being in ecclesiastical use' if it was, in fact, being demolished.

The question then arises as to what constitutes partial demolition. Can a major part of a church be demolished without consent on the grounds that part of it remains in ecclesiastical use?

SAVE, on the advice of its lawyers, has repeatedly taken the view, with successful results, that if any work of demolition, although not total, is sufficiently substantial to alter or remove the identity of the building, then listed building consent is required.

If, therefore, you are faced with a threat to a listed church of this kind, contact SAVE immediately.

Case History
CHURCH OF ST FRANCIS XAVIER, LIVERPOOL

WHEN IS A church not a church? This is a question SAVE has repeatedly had to consider.

The position on partial demolition, however, remained uncertain after the House of Lords case, and by degrees various church bodies began to put forward proposals for partial demolition, in some cases leaving no more than a facade or church hall, arguing that, as part of the site was to remain in ecclesiastical use, no permission to demolish was required.

SAVE took up this issue with the case of St Francis Xavier in Liverpool. Here, the Catholic Church authorities had decided to retain no more than the spire and the lady chapel, demolishing the whole body

SAVE ACTION GUIDE

of the church. SAVE's solicitors argued that the House of Lords judgment 'extends to the case where the demolition, although not total, is sufficiently substantial to alter or remove the identity of the building'.

Church of St Francis Xavier, Liverpool. SAVE argued successfully that listed building consent was required for partial demolition

CHURCHES

The chapel, SAVE contended, represented no more than one sixth of the overall floor space and was a later addition. 'Even assuming a genuine ecclesiastic use of the chapel following demolition of the remainder, it cannot be said the church as such is still in ecclesiastical use or would be but for the works.' The reference in the House of Lords case to partial demolition, the letter continued, is 'limited to works which leave the identity of the original building substantially intact'.

Unless they received an assurance, within twenty-one days, that the trustees of the church would not proceed until listed building consent had been obtained, our solicitors would seek leave of the Attorney General to bring proceedings for a declaration that listed building consent was required.

Two weeks later a letter arrived from the solicitors for the archdiocese providing the assurance that we sought.

Very soon afterwards, the archdiocese withdrew its plans and the church thankfully continues in use.

Demolition in conservation areas

Permission is also needed to demolish an unlisted church in a conservation area. There are many churches, pleasant or handsome, which though not perhaps of special architectural interest, are none the less important and well-loved local landmarks. Permission is needed to demolish such buildings and this provides the opportunity to investigate suitable alternative uses. Experience shows that there are a wide range of uses that preserve the landmark value of the building while providing a necessary investment for its adaptation.

Finding a suitable use

The best alternative use is likely to be one that not only leaves the exterior of the building unchanged, but one that involves minimal subdivision of the interior.

Concert halls, arts centres or community centres, if sympathetically designed, are probably the most appropriate, but these are likely to depend on grants or donations, and most towns will not require more than one of any one type.

In SAVE's experience, one of the best alternatives is a careful conversion into an open-plan office. Office use can allow the church interior to remain undivided. Pews will have to be removed but if furniture is arranged in an orderly, symmetrical fashion it responds to the architectural layout of the building. Galleries can provide further working space out of sight. Features such as the organ case, pulpit (or rostrum in a Nonconformist chapel) can remain, as well as the monuments on the walls and sometimes some of the stained glass. If the chancel or east end is self-contained, it can possibly be left substantially intact.

SAVE ACTION GUIDE

Case History

CHURCH OF THE HOLY NAME, MANCHESTER

A MAGNIFICENT CATHOLIC church of 1869–71 by Joseph Hansom (designer of the Hansom cab), the Church of the Holy Name has a most spectacular interior which, despite its elaborate fittings and furnishings, has a beautifully light and airy atmosphere.

The large and thriving congregation was stunned by the Jesuits' sudden announcement, in March 1989, that they were to close and sell off the church on the open market—'for any reasonable use', according the sale particulars. The congregation, as the Friends of the Holy Name, contacted SAVE for help. Our first step was to get the Department of the Environment to upgrade the building to II* in recognition of its remarkable interior. Secondly, we set about drawing attention, nationally and locally, to a threatened church that simply could not be described as being redundant, having a weekly congregation of over 1,500 worshippers!

Although SAVE believes that alternative uses are possible for most types of buildings, including churches, the Holy Name was an exception and our fears for its future increased with rumours of purchase offers from McDonald's. After persistent lobbying of the Bishop of Salford and correspondence with the Jesuits, they agreed to withdraw the church from sale, and worship now continues as before.

Church of the Holy Name, Manchester. Despite a thriving congregation, the church was to be closed and sold off 'for any reasonable use'. Public protest helped to prevent this and worship now continues as before

CHURCHES

Nonconformist churches and chapels

'As nasty a thing as I've looked at for many a day', says one of the characters in Trollope's *Vicar of Bullhampton* of the local Nonconformist chapel.

Old prejudices die hard and it is only very recently that chapels have been noticed at all in guide books or architectural histories. Very few were included in the initial lists of historic buildings and as a result a very large number have been demolished.

From the start, chapels have been a constant source of concern to SAVE, and Northern chapel architecture was the subject of a special SAVE exhibition and report, *The Fall of Zion*.

All the Nonconformist denominations—the Baptists, the Congregationalists (now the United Reformed Church), the Methodists, the Quakers, the Unitarians as well as smaller denominations such as the Countess of Huntingdon's Connexion—have interesting and often remarkable buildings.

Chapels are not only local landmarks—as much part of the character of any town as the post office or the railway station—they almost always repay a visit inside.

Unlike parish churches, they are rarely open except at service times, so if ever you see the door of a chapel open—when it is being cleaned or the organist is practising—be sure to go inside. You will always be welcomed, but the real surprise is to see how beautifully most chapels are kept. Many are also remarkably unaltered, retaining original pews and galleries, often in an intriguing horseshoe layout, with the traditional arrangement of central pulpit and special rostrum for the elders.

The first battle has been to ensure that chapels are listed, the second to secure grants for repairs. These are now available from English Heritage. Chapels may be eligible in their own right if they are outstanding buildings (grade I or II*), or on townscape grounds if they are in conservation areas.

Many chapel congregations are small or elderly, and the burden of maintaining them, let alone carrying out major repairs, with fast-dwindling resources, may seem insuperable.

However, it may be possible to make a case for a higher proportion of grant aid if the resources available are very limited.

Many chapels have an important asset in the form of substantial ancillary accommodation. This may be underneath the chapel, or behind or beside it, and may consist of a church hall, meeting rooms and offices. Such accommodation can often be let on a long lease or sold to raise a capital sum. Alternatively, where the chapel is too large, the congregation may move into the church hall, freeing the chapel for a different use.

In looking at alternative uses, the first question is to decide how much of the interior it is desirable or practical to preserve. If possible preference should be given to the proposal that maintains the interior as an undivided

SAVE ACTION GUIDE

space. If the pews are an essential part of the design, this will probably limit the choice of uses—maybe as a concert hall, conference and lecture hall, or simply as a show place. If the pews can be removed without incurring too much damage, a large area of floor space will become available for a range of activities—open-plan office use may be one of the most profitable and least damaging. In such cases as the United Reformed Church at Headingley Hill, Leeds, it has proved possible to retain not only the galleries and organ, but also the pulpit and rostrum arrangement at the west end.

A first move in such cases is to establish which alternative uses will be acceptable to the local planning authority. Bear in mind that the Department of the Environment has guidelines encouraging local planners to be flexible about change of use where this may help to provide a new lease of life for a problem listed building.

While substantial fees are now payable for planning applications relative to the size of the building, the charge for a simple change of use may be a smaller fixed fee. Where the minister and elders of a church have decided to pursue an application for demolition, remember they may only have come to this decision as a last resort, perhaps having received advice that there was no possibility of alternative use.

In such cases, try to make contact with individual trustees, who may be sympathetic and listen. Then seek an opportunity for a meeting. This is the time to bring your own professional advisors—a local architect, engineer, surveyor or quantity surveyor—with special knowledge of historic buildings.

United Reformed Church, Headingley Hill, Leeds. A good conversion to office use, **right**, the exterior, **left**, remains unaltered

CHURCHES

At the meeting, the most important point to convey is that your alternative proposals need not be to their detriment, either in financial terms or in the provision of any accommodation they may be hoping for in a new development on the site. Be sure to understand their needs and aspirations and counterbalance any pessimistic reports they may have received about the church's condition and the cost of repair.

Case History
EAST STREET METHODIST CHAPEL, TONBRIDGE, KENT

THOUGH THIS PLEASANT little chapel in a quiet side street was clearly suitable for conversion to offices—providing the trustees with the financial return they sought—the story was that it had to be demolished because there was nowhere to site the requisite number of car-parking spaces. SAVE challenged this, succeeded in getting the building listed and argued that the building could be used as an extension for a nearby office that already had on-site car-parking.

The Church in Wales

The Anglican Church in Wales possesses a remarkable number of medieval churches. No less important in terms of architecture, landscape and Welsh history are the many thousands of Nonconformist chapels.

Following disestablishment in 1923, the Church in Wales has been quite independent of the Church of England. There is no formal procedure, like the Pastoral Measure, for declaring unwanted churches redundant and deciding their future. And there is no Redundant Churches Fund to take on responsibility for outstanding churches that need to be preserved intact, complete with their furnishings.

The problem has become acute with the decision of the Welsh Synod that up to half of the Anglican churches in Wales may be closed. These buildings are not large or ornate; they were usually very sturdily built to withstand the elements; the roofs normally have stone slates; and the walls are plain, with little ornamental carving and few mouldings.

The position of these churches remains unclear. If services are no longer to be held, even irregularly, there may still be a local farmer or former parishioner who is willing to carry out basic maintenance.

One interesting idea has been put forward by Stephen Weeks who lives in Wales and has restored Penhow Castle. He has a scheme to take over a small number of simple churches and adapt them as retreats. They would be let to people who, for one reason or another, wanted to spend some time in the country away from the pressures of the modern world and are prepared to live very simply. These people would undertake to read a daily service and carry out a rota of chores.

SAVE ACTION GUIDE

Yerbeston Church, Dyfed. An abandoned Welsh church with potential for re-use

With chapels, the problems are more acute. Many of these are major landmarks rising high above surrounding houses, but often they are far too large for present congregations. Once maintenance ceases, it is not long before the roof starts to leak, the plasterwork or the ceiling to become stained and damaged, and dry rot to take hold.

The need is for vigilance, by the local planners as well as by interested local people. It need not cost much to replace a slate or clean a gutter. And if this is not done the repair bill will escalate dramatically.

Fortunately, the importance and individuality of chapel architecture is now being recognized, thanks to the work of writers and teachers such as John Hilling and Professor Anthony Jones, of the Texas Christian University, who has spent numerous summers visiting and photographing chapels. The chapels are often temple-form buildings with pediments and columns, and the use of the orders is often bold and unusual, with an intriguing disregard for the rules.

The Church in Scotland

Scotland, compared to England and Wales, has relatively few medieval churches but, precisely because so many were destroyed at the time of the Reformation, Scotland is rich in seventeenth- and eighteenth-century ecclesiastical architecture.

The nineteenth and early twentieth centuries saw a remarkable bout of church building, fuelled by the great split in 1843 when 451 out of a total of 1,203 ministers left to form the Free Church of Scotland. Thus every town in Scotland, and in some places every parish, had a Church of Scotland

CHURCHES

Gilcomston Church, Aberdeen. The loss of the spire would have dramatically altered the skyline of the city. The Historic Buildings Council for Scotland gave a major grant of £1.1 million so that the spire could be dismantled and rebuilt. This was the largest grant ever offered by the HBCS, but many other churches faced with closure because of a repair crisis have also received substantial aid from the Council

SAVE ACTION GUIDE

church, a Free church, an Episcopalian church and possibly a Roman Catholic, Methodist or Baptist church as well.

Scotland's churches are of special value for three reasons. First, many are designed by notable Scottish architects; second, many contain remarkably complete and unaltered interiors; and third, thanks to prominent towers and spires, most play a major role in the townscape.

Though church attendance in Scotland is remarkably strong, there has been a steady stream of closures ever since the Church of Scotland and the United Free Church came together again in 1929. As a result, numerous important churches, particularly in Glasgow, have been demolished.

However, the Historic Buildings Council for Scotland has increasingly been able to give some very substantial grants towards churches, ensuring that churches faced with closure because of a repairs crisis have been able to continue in use. Major grants have been given to churches for their townscape value as well as for their intrinsic architectural importance. The largest grant ever offered was £1.1 million for the Gilcomston Church in Aberdeen—to cover the cost of dismantling and rebuilding the spire. The justification for this was that it saved the skyline of the Granite City.

⑦ TOWN BUILDINGS

THE MOST FREQUENT threat is to quite modest buildings in town centres. The proposal may be to replace just a single building or a row of shops, or there may be plans for a comprehensive redevelopment involving a whole block or more.

Yet these more modest buildings are as important to the character of a town as the architecturally outstanding ones. Almost always they can be modernized and adapted: the developer simply believes that a new building will be worth more.

Ironically, very often it is conservation policies, successfully applied over a period of time, that have made the centre a more attractive investment to owners and increased the value of properties. The result is that they are bought up by development companies, insurance companies and pension funds looking to maximize their value.

Experience shows that shopping habits change radically in character every ten to twenty years. The big supermarkets, or what seemed big supermarkets then, which disfigured numerous high streets in the 1960s, have now been replaced by a much larger generation of stores. The life of a new shopping precinct may be no more than twenty years.

Two cardinal points must be borne in mind. First, any new shopping development should not only respect the character of the town but should also, as far as possible, be reversible—that is, relatively easily removed when it is no longer needed. And second, it must be conceived and laid out in such a way as to support existing shops and shopping streets.

Arguments such as these will weigh strongly with an inspector at a public inquiry, and there are numerous examples of local civic trusts and amenity societies working with local architects and surveyors to put up alternative schemes that will be far less damaging to their town.

SAVE itself has prepared a number of such schemes for Billingsgate Market, the No 1 Poultry site opposite the Bank of England and for Spitalfields Market, all in the City of London.

SAVE ACTION GUIDE

The essential need when a proposed redevelopment poses a threat is to rally popular support. The local authority may be hesitant as to the merit of the buildings and be worried whether the Department of the Environment will support it if there is an appeal—often a lengthy and expensive procedure.

The most straightforward way of demonstrating the strength of local feeling is through a petition. It only takes two or three volunteers on a busy market day or Saturday afternoon to gather several hundred signatures. One of the classic instances is Chesterfield, where the town had entered a partnership with a property company to build over the city's open-air market place, replacing it with a covered market, shops and offices. More than 80,000 people signed the petition and brought the scheme to a halt.

Obviously, it will be a great bonus if you can win the support of local shopkeepers. Very often shopping schemes are aimed principally at the multiple chains, which will pay higher rents. Unfortunately, the profits they will make will not help the local economy. Existing shops and businesses, if they are to be relocated, may be offered accommodation that is smaller, less well placed or more expensive.

If at all possible, start the campaign while shops are still occupied: once boarded up, they will be perceived by some as an eyesore—though many buildings in this state have been saved and brought back into use.

Clearly there is a need in most towns for increased and improved shopping facilities and there is a danger that, if it is not provided in some form, there will be pressure for major developments outside town or on the outskirts. These, if they proceed on a large scale, can have the damaging effect of taking custom away from the town centre on a substantial scale. Many provincial towns in the United States have lost almost all their shops to suburban shopping malls and have become very dead places as a result.

In Britain, there are two principal alternatives that have been proved to work on many occasions. The first is to build the new shopping mall or supermarket immediately adjacent to the town centre. Most towns have a former industrial area close to the centre—it may be a railway goods yard, cattle market or former brewery—which offers ample space for car-parking as well as large areas for shops. The important thing is that it is within walking distance of the centre. People coming to shop in the supermarket can then walk into town and patronize the smaller food shops, boutiques and speciality stores.

The second alternative is to slot the new development in behind existing frontages. Efforts should be made to preserve not just the facades but a substantial part of the interior as well, and possibly the whole building. Premises 'over the shop', looking on to the town's main streets, can provide desirable offices for local professional firms, or indeed flats—residential use in particular keeps the streets alive in the evenings and at weekends when the shops are shut.

TOWN BUILDINGS

Shopping developments within towns are of two principal kinds nowadays —covered or open. The tendency is to press for covered shopping malls, but there are many examples of attractive small courtyards and squares that open up behind existing streets and that are busy and popular spaces.

It is important to try to preserve some of the old pedestrian routes through the new precinct. This may be of advantage to the developer too, attracting passers-by, even though they may initially be looking for a short cut. Some of the disastrous shopping centres of the 1960s suffered greatly from under-use because of limited public access from the surrounding streets.

If the new mall is to be covered, probably the best option is for it to be glazed in the manner of the arcades which cut through many nineteenth-century blocks.

A number of good new shopping developments have commissioned works from local artists and sculptors, using stained glass, decorative ironwork, fountains and other features. This gives an image far removed from those bleak, concrete areas with a few hard benches and overflowing litter bins that they will hopefully replace.

Lamb and Lion Yard, Farnham, Surrey. A well-designed new shopping centre makes an attractive feature within the town

SAVE ACTION GUIDE

Preservation Pays

The cost of preserving historic buildings is often presented as a massive burden to the taxpayer.

SAVE's report, *Preservation Pays*, set out to document the very substantial economic benefits that accrued through tourism, both to commerce and to the exchequer.

Statistics available from numerous British Tourist Authority surveys showed that history and tradition—in other words, heritage—formed the prime attraction for overseas visitors. Even assigning a conservative twenty-five per cent of earnings in 1977 to heritage, this showed historic buildings and areas were responsible for earning at least £500 million in foreign exchange.

Again at the minimum, £60 million of this accrued directly to central government through VAT and duty on petrol, liquor and cigarettes (this was at a time when VAT was eight per cent, not the current fifteen per cent). By contrast, the total amount available in grants from the Historic Buildings Council for England in 1970–78 was £4.6 million. Even this sum was comfortably exceeded by the sums the Government received in VAT on repairs to historic buildings. At the time, VAT on repairs to churches and cathedrals alone totalled an estimated £1.6 million a year.

SAVE also carried out research in individual historic towns, in some cases professionally, in others with the help of local civic societies. This was important in demonstrating the extent to which revenue and profits were locally maintained. No less than eighty-five per cent of the catering and retail outlets and eighty-four per cent of the accommodation establishments were found to be locally owned in the six locations where detailed research was done: Arundel, Broadway, Chipping Campden, Lavenham, Long Melford and Woodstock.

Other research demonstrated that should Canterbury Cathedral collapse in some dreadful calamity, it would actually pay the city to rebuild it. Surveys showed that ninety-three per cent of Canterbury's tourists visited or intended to visit the Cathedral. Max Hanna, an economist at the English Tourist Board who was joint author of SAVE's *Preservation Pays*, calculated that the preservation of the Cathedral was then worth £5 million gross income, or £1.5 million net, each year to the local economy.

Case History
BRACKEN HOUSE, LONDON

BRACKEN HOUSE, THE former home of the *Financial Times*, came under threat at the time ministers were considering the introduction of the Thirty Year Rule on listing (see page 149), and probably played a major part in securing the greater protection for post-war buildings of excellence that SAVE had sought for so long.

TOWN BUILDINGS

Bracken House in the City of London. A model of Michael Hopkins' design retaining the outer elements of the listed building with a newly designed inner core

We wrote to the minister, William Waldegrave, in the autumn of 1986 requesting the spotlisting of Bracken House—in our view (shared by the Thirties Society) one of the most remarkable post-war buildings in London.

It was designed by Sir Albert Richardson ('the last of the Georgians') in 1955–59 and in style and use of materials—pinkish brick, reflecting the pages of the *FT*, bronze window and door frames, and copper cornicing and roof—it was a clear rejection of the Modern movement of the time.

The *FT* was moving premises and sold the building to a Japanese Corporation for £143 million—the highest price ever paid for a City site. They announced plans for its complete redevelopment and applied for a certificate of immunity of listing.

Despite repeated letters from SAVE, the Department of the Environment refused to make a decision on whether or not to list the building. Finally, in August 1987, SAVE wrote a firm and formal letter to the Secretary of State stating that, if the Department refused to list the building, SAVE would consider taking legal action. As in previous cases, we believed he was failing to carry out his statutory duties.

Within a week, we received a letter back from the minister informing us that Bracken House had been listed grade II*. It was the first post-war building in England to be listed and a considerable victory for the conservation movement.

The new owners of the building, instead of continuing with demolition plans, instructed their architect, Michael Hopkins, to produce a scheme retaining the outer shell of Bracken House with a new core. The result is an exciting and innovative marriage of the old and the new, and a widely acclaimed architectural success.

SAVE ACTION GUIDE

Case History

MANSION HOUSE SQUARE AND THE NO I POULTRY SITE, LONDON

SAVE'S MOST CELEBRATED and prolonged battle has been to stop the demolition of the important triangle of Victorian buildings in the heart of the City of London that includes Mappin and Webb, Mansion House and the Bank of England.

The buildings date from the 1870s and are recognized as one of the best, if not the best, surviving groups of commercial buildings of that time. The range of architectural styles, with details such as terracotta friezes, gargoyles and ironwork, the attractive pub and wine bar, and the two medieval lanes that run through the site, with street-level shops all around the perimeter of the buildings, are what makes the City a unique place.

The Bank conservation area is arguably the most sensitive conservation area in the country in terms of the colossal pressures on it, and the implications for listed buildings and conservation areas everywhere—should demolition be permitted—are extremely worrying. That is why, in its efforts to preserve the buildings and uphold the general presumption in favour of historic buildings that exists within the law, SAVE has had to argue its case all the way to the House of Lords.

We have had enormous public support: people donated help or money and wrote letters to the City, to the public inquiry inspectors, to the Secretary of State and to the developers.

The story begins in the 1960s, when property magnate Peter Palumbo (now a leading public figure in the arts world) began purchasing the freeholds of all the buildings on the site. His dream was to build on the site a building by the Modernist architect Mies van der Rohe, which would also create a New York-style plaza, to be known as Mansion House Square. This new arrangement and the tall glass structure of Mies's pure and austere design would irrevocably alter the character of that part of the City. SAVE and many others (including the Prince of Wales who compared the proposed building to 'a glass stump better suited to downtown Chicago') believed the new scheme would be simply disastrous.

SAVE has consistently held the view that the buildings on the site should be refurbished to provide shops and offices of a superior quality. Early on, we commissioned the architect Terry Farrell to draw up a scheme showing exactly this. The Farrell scheme has been a vital weapon in the battle, showing how important it is to put forward alternative but practical uses for a threatened site.

A lengthy public inquiry ensued in 1984 with expert witnesses on both sides. Mr Palumbo assembled a formidable team of architects and planners. Likewise, the SAVE team was a wealth of talent and expertise. The difference was that these professionals were giving their time for free.

TOWN BUILDINGS

A year later, the Secretary of State for the Environment, then Patrick Jenkin, accepted his inspector's recommendations that the Mies scheme should not be given consent. There was much cheering in the conservationist camp.

But not for long. Determined to achieve his ambition of a modern building on the site, the developer went to a second architect, James Stirling, for a new design. However, when unveiled, this scheme met with only a lukewarm response (and was disparagingly described by the Prince of Wales as 'resembling a 1930s wireless set') and SAVE renewed its objection at a second public inquiry in 1988.

Facing opposition from the City, from English Heritage and all the conservation groups, amenity organizations and civic societies in the country, as well as hundreds of people who work in the City, it was quite a shock when a different Environment Secretary, Nicholas Ridley, agreeing with his inspector, granted permission for demolition and redevelopment.

SAVE wasted no time in seeking legal advice as to whether the decision could be challenged. Encouraged by the views of our solicitor, David Cooper of Gouldens, Robert Carnwath, QC appeared on SAVE's behalf seeking to quash Ridley's decision on the grounds that he gave insufficient and unclear reasons for granting consent.

The case was heard in December 1989. We lost, but appealed and came to the Court of Appeal in March 1990. This time, Ridley's decision was quashed; the three Appeal Judges agreed that if a minister departed from a clearly stated policy he had to explain why — something Ridley had failed to do in this case.

However, when the case was brought before the House of Lords in 1991, Lord Bridge disagreed, concluding that the decision letter had been based entirely on the 'special circumstances of the case' and that, contrary to SAVE's fears, no dangerous precedent would be set. In our view, though, every developer believes his own particular case to be unique, with 'special circumstances' to consider; and every developer will seek to demolish existing listed buildings by arguing that they will be replaced by a much better piece of architecture.

Case History
PITT STREET BATHS, PORTSMOUTH

THESE BATHS WERE turned into a handsome Edwardian Arts and Crafts complex after they were suddenly vacated by the Navy. The building was in good condition, but the city council wished to clear the site to make way for yet another comprehensive shopping development of the kind that has already blighted other parts of the city beyond recall. Finding a new use for a swimming pool is not easy, though they can be floored over as sports halls. Hampshire County Council then proposed to reopen the baths as a much-needed facility for local people living in nearby tower blocks.

⑧ INTERIORS

IT IS OBVIOUS that the interiors of many historic buildings are at least as fine and significant as their exteriors. The problem is that the early lists of historic buildings were done at such a pace that they had to be assessed largely on the basis of their exteriors. Even as the lists have been revised and filled out, inspectors have no right of access to examine interiors. Partly as a result, the discovery of interior features unknown to the inspector is accepted by the Department of the Environment as a reason for spotlisting.

Equally, many people, including owners, developers and even some planners, continue to believe that it is only the exterior of the building, or at least a grade II building, that is protected by listing. This is not the case. Any work which materially affects the character of a listed building, inside or out, requires listed building consent.

When listed buildings are subject to major refurbishment, especially in historic towns, it is important that the local planning officer and the local civic society are aware of the interior and have examined it to see what features may be worth retaining.

Many so-called 'refurbishments', particularly of buildings in town centres, are very radical. The reason is not simply that the developer has little experience of historic buildings, but that the pension fund or insurance company buying it wants a building which is effectively new, with a sure life of many years ahead of it. This leads to an 'if in doubt, take it out' approach. Floors needing strengthening are simply replaced, and because fine old panelling is thought to be infested with every imaginable beetle permission is obtained to strip it out and replace it in replica.

In other cases, interior fittings may be stripped out illegally. If this happens, it is important that local authorities prosecute. In the past, it often seemed that the fines were too small to be effective—the maximum fine a magistrates court can impose is £2,000. But recently, the City of Westminster successfully prosecuted both an owner and builder, who had

INTERIORS

stripped out large quantities of fine panelling from an early eighteenth-century house in Soho, on a total of no less than fourteen charges. The court imposed the maximum fine on each charge and also demanded complete reinstatement. This represents a very substantial penalty and will undoubtedly make other owners and builders much more cautious over alterations.

It has also to be recognized that all owners may need to make alterations and improvements to their property from time to time. If done well, these can add an interesting chapter to the history of the building, as they have done in the past. If such alterations have been well thought out, and the detail carefully considered, it must be desirable that the proposals receive support and are passed with as little fuss as possible. Maintaining a historic building is a considerable responsibility and the task should not be made unnecessarily daunting or frustrating by too much interference over small things.

Case History
THE THREE GRACES, WOBURN ABBEY, BEDFORDSHIRE

CANOVA'S 'THREE GRACES' was the most important piece of neoclassical sculpture in Britain.

It was commissioned from the sculptor by the sixth Duke of Bedford and, once transported from Rome, housed in the Temple of the Graces specially built for it at Woburn.

When it was loaned for 'The Treasure Houses of Britain' exhibition in Washington, it was assumed that, like all the other works of art on show, it would be returned to its original setting. In fact, though the statue was exhibited as the property of the Marquess of Tavistock and the Bedford Estate Trustees, it had already been sold to a Cayman Island company, Fine Art Investment and Display Limited. When, three years later, a licence was sought by the Getty Museum for its export, SAVE pressed the local authority to serve an enforcement notice requiring the return of the statue to its plinth in the grade I listed building from which it had been removed.

The local planners considered the matter seriously, but in the end the officer's recommendation was rejected by the committee. SAVE had meanwhile expressed its concern to the Department of the Environment and received an intimation that the ministers might consider serving an enforcement notice if the local authority demurred.

The local authority decision not to take action coincided with the expiry of the export stop on the statue. Suddenly, the position was desperate. Thanks to support from the Prince of Wales, the export stop was extended; but then came a knee blow. Department of the Environment ministers

SAVE ACTION GUIDE

'The Three Graces', Woburn Abbey, Bedfordshire. The issue in this case was whether or not listed building consent should have been obtained before the neoclassical statue was removed from the Temple of Graces, a listed building specifically designed to house it

announced that though they had been advised that the statue was part of the listed building, and that consent was therefore required for its removal, they none the less considered it was a chattel, and would not take enforcement action.

INTERIORS

In SAVE's view this decision was self-contradictory and made a nonsense of the law, so SAVE immediately set about investigating the possibility of legal action. Meanwhile, the Victoria and Albert Museum secured the agreement of the owners to the loan of the statue while an appeal was launched to raise funds to match the Getty offer of £7.6 million.

We published a lightning report, *Save the Woburn Canova*, quoting golden opinions of the statue from leading luminaries of the arts; but it soon became evident that the chances of raising the necessary funds were very slim. By this time, however, SAVE had received permission for judicial review of the ministers' decision and suddenly the picture changed entirely.

Ministers none the less were now concerned to save the statue by different means; and early in the spring of 1989, Nicholas Ridley announced a change in the rules governing the export of works of art, by which private purchasers, as well as public institutions, could purchase works subject to an export stop. With this came the news that the Barclay brothers had offered to buy the statue and were proposing to put it on show alternately in the V & A and the National Gallery of Scotland.

This announcement met with considerable antipathy from Fine Art Investment and Display, and it rapidly became clear that the company would be unlikely to sell to the Barclay brothers. None the less, the Barclay offer had been instrumental in saving the statue for the nation at least for the time being and, soon after, the Minister for the Arts announced that an export licence had been refused.

As SAVE arrived in court, with Robert Carnwath as QC and Gouldens as solicitors, there was a new, unexpected twist in the saga. Treasury Counsel announced that the Secretary of State for the Environment was now inclined to take the view that the statue was not part of the listed building, and so asked for an adjournment. Recognizing that this was a complete change of view on the part of ministers, he undertook on their behalf that the Secretary of State would reconsider the whole question of listing and re-determine the issue.

SAVE, supported by English Heritage, promptly submitted a powerful statement supporting the case for considering the statue as a fixture, the removal of which would profoundly affect the character of the listed building. It is a measure of the seriousness of the arguments we put that, more than six months later, the Department still failed to issue the ruling, which it had promised to deliver as a matter of some urgency.

⑨ PRESERVING FACADES

STRONG FEELINGS ARE held on the pros and cons of facadism—keeping the outer (normally just the front) skin of a building and rebuilding behind. Purists may have an essential moral objection that this approach is false—what Ruskin or Morris would have called a lie. Certainly many interiors that have been gutted or scooped out in this way would now be considered worthy of retention—notably many of Nash's interiors around Regent's Park.

What seems commonplace today may be of great interest to the next generation. Even when a building is relatively plain inside, as time passes all historic finishes and fabric are seen to be of greater significance; so it is desirable to preserve as much of the original interior as possible.

All existing buildings should also be seen as a potential resource. Demolishing them simply to rebuild, albeit in an almost identical form, involves the consumption of substantial raw materials and energy and never quite captures the spirit of the building that stood there before.

However, it has to be recognized that the whole concept of conservation areas would never have become established in many places without a willingness by local authorities to accept development behind facades. Retention of street frontages is a trade-off developers have been willing to accept in return for planning permission.

There is, moreover, increasing recognition of the value of street architecture. Most streets are essentially a collection of frontages, and the street scene has an existence to some extent independent of the buildings behind it, enjoyed by numerous people who never enter the buildings. A facade has a function as an ornament to a town as well as cloaking a building.

The worry, of course, is that the next time around the owner will say, 'It's not worth preserving—it's just a facade.' A building adapted or retained in its totality can have many lives; keeping just the facade might prolong its life by no more than twenty years. But if the importance of a facade to a street has been recognized once, the argument that it is worth retaining for its contribution to the townscape must be upheld.

PRESERVING FACADES

For this reason it is vital that the new structure behind the facade is designed so that it can be dismantled without damaging the earlier structure.

Case History
GUILDHALL SCHOOL OF MUSIC, LONDON

THIS BUILDING, WITH its exceptionally fine stone carving, came near to being demolished in 1980. A joint scheme, by developers Trafalgar House and Wimpey, proposed a massive new building between Tudor Street and the Embankment near Blackfriars. Although they proposed retaining the City of London Boys' School on the Embankment, all buildings behind, including the School of Music, would be swept away.

Built between 1885 and 1897, the earliest part of the Music School was designed by Sir Horace Jones (the Billingsgate architect). Its great attraction was the exquisite quality of the stone carving, with festoons of musical trophies and elegantly decorated *oeil de boeuf* windows.

SAVE voiced loud objections. Following the recent and much-lamented demolition of the Firestone Factory by Trafalgar House, we pressed successfully for the listing of the School of Music. At the same time we wrote to Trafalgar House, pleading that the School be retained. The reply was hardly encouraging. However, six months later the scheme was revised. It was decided to keep the marvellous facades of the School of Music and build anew within them.

Guildhall School of Music, London. The decorative facade has been incorporated into the redevelopment

SAVE ACTION GUIDE

Case History
ST GEORGE'S HOSPITAL, LONDON

WILLIAM WILKINS' GREEK Revival hospital overlooking Hyde Park Corner is unquestionably one of London's most familiar landmarks. The problem SAVE faced was that it had been so disfigured by later alterations that many people doubted it was of sufficient interest to merit saving. However, SAVE took the view that the hospital formed an important set piece of Regency townscape, being not only at a focal point in the middle of the royal parks, but also adjacent to both Decimus Burton's Ionic arch at the entrance to Hyde Park and Apsley House.

Once SAVE's case for the significance of the building was made, its retention as part of the London scene was accepted by all the parties involved. Internally, the only significant architectural feature was the two-storey entrance hall, and this is to be retained. The rest of the interior had been very much altered over the years and little original work of consequence remained visible.

The solution therefore has been to agree a change of use for the Wilkins building—to a hotel—with an office development behind. This agreement was reached in the face of major pressure from the Health Authority, the Grosvenor Estate and the developer, to ensure the best return from the site. But within this context, Wilkins' elegant stuccoed facades will be retained, and an important landmark has been saved and will look far more handsome and dignified than it has for many years.

⑩ SHOPFRONTS

MANY OF BRITAIN'S historic towns are, and have long been, dominated by shops and shopping. Although traditional shopfronts add charm and individuality to high streets, unprecedented damage has been done over the last century. SAVE's report, *The Scourge of Britain's High Streets*, set out to provide a visual record of the damage, canvas the views of those on the spot (i.e. local planning officers and civic societies), and find examples of successful sensitive treatment. The report's opening blast began:

> 'Thou shalt conform', is the new commandment of the national organizations which dominate high streets all over Britain. Diversity, individuality and regional character are out. Standardized fascias and fronts, company colours, house lettering and stylized logos are in with a vengeance. This coarseness of imagery—particularly crude colours and alien materials—is visually impoverishing our towns at appalling speed. Everywhere, high streets are looking more and more alike. Though done with the intention of establishing a virile, distinctive presence, the effect is usually to reduce shopping centres to an unprecedented level of blandness and monotony.
>
> The problem is twofold. Firstly, there is the intrusion of ill-designed new buildings in sensitive parts of the high street: buildings which are too high and too wide, which break with traditional floor levels and introduce large dead areas over the shopface.
>
> Secondly, there is the mutilation of existing buildings by the imposition of unsuitable standard fascias and the insertion of curtain glass windows leaving upper storeys floating in mid-air.
>
> All too rarely is the building considered as a whole: the shopfront is applied without a thought as to whether it clashes or blends in colour, proportion, materials or design with the building above. Nor is this just a problem that is eating away the character of historic towns and conservation areas. Almost every high street in Britain has some

glimmer of character which can be brought out sensitively rather than needlessly brutalized.

For too long, local planning authorities and local civic societies have been fighting an uneven battle against strong-arm tactics by the multiples. Chain stores will threaten to take their business to another town if planners do not accept standard formulae. Their architects or estates departments will quote the precedent of mutilated buildings nearby as justification for allowing another unsuitable, unsympathetic design which will result in further erosion of the town's character.

National organizations, which should in fact be setting an example in good sensitive design and leading the way in enhancing the urban environment, are all too often blind to local needs.

Two principal culprits emerged. First, those firms with in-house architects, which insist on a standard formula without consideration of local conditions. Second, the shopfitting firms or specialist sign creators.

In a second report, SAVE produced a charter for shopfronts. This has been adapted by numerous local planning authorities, many of whom have produced their own leaflets laying down specific guidelines and illustrating examples of good and bad practice. The conservation area legislation also gives local planners a stronger degree of control over shopfronts than any other part of the building or type of building.

In considering shopfronts, the first need is to ensure that existing ones of character are preserved and sympathetically treated. Even the simplest nineteenth-century shopfront will be attractively decorated. In other cases, original cornice detail may survive intact behind a box fascia—this is often the case in turn-of-the-century shopping parades.

Good paint schemes and carefully chosen lettering should be your first option. Where damage has been done, particularly in gouging out a shopfront and leaving fine brick or stone upper storeys suspended over a vast area of plate glass, it may be worth seeking reinstatement. Old photographs or postcards will often survive, showing the original detail. The years around 1900 were the golden age of shopfront design. Virtually any Arts and Crafts or Art Nouveau building can be assumed to have had a highly elaborate shopfront beneath.

The effect of reinstatement would be dramatic, bringing back numerous fine buildings as focal points in the street scene. The appeal of traditional shopfronts in purely commercial terms is also apparent in new developments, where historic styles are often used to promote a bespoke image.

By the same token, there is a need for good new shopfront design that is highly individual in style but respects the character of the buildings above and beside it. In Vienna, the architect Hans Hollein has produced small new shopfronts that are a sensation; so there is no reason why appropriately sited new shopfronts, in a contemporary or even futuristic style, cannot sometimes add zip to a high street.

SHOPFRONTS

49–51 Cookridge Street, Leeds. After a long battle, these old buildings, **above**, have been restored, **below**, and retain all their original features

⑾ STREET FURNITURE

MUCH OF THE character and charm of cities, towns and villages derives from good street furniture. Too much of it, however, is thoughtlessly neglected or replaced, often at great expense.

It needs to be recognized that it is the surface of any street or pavement that provides its essential character. If you walk into a medieval parish church, the sight and feel of an old stone floor will immediately tell you that here is a church that has been spared the restorer's hand.

All old stone paving slabs deserve retention, as do granite kerbs. Beneath the tarmac in many old streets and lanes, the original stone sets or cobbles survive and can be exposed. Whatever happens, try to protect these stone sets from being dug up and thrown away. Like the archaeology under the ground, they are a resource for the future. Look carefully at the pavement as there are many details that tell a story. Coal hole covers were made in different patterns and embossed with the name of the foundry; outside older houses, the bootscrapers can often still be seen.

Many categories of street furniture can now be listed—pillar boxes, telephone kiosks, drinking fountains and bus shelters. Though the traditional pillar boxes—oval, round or octagonal—appear at the moment safe, the wall-mounted variety are under threat. Due to public outcry, well over 1,000 (out of perhaps 50,000) red telephone boxes have been listed, but this of course is only a tiny fraction. The need is to protect and retain those that are landmarks. A red telephone box on a village green is part of the country scene, as quintessential in its way as the village pond or pub. A red telephone box in such circumstances may not be special in itself, but special to the area.

Great care was taken in the early years of this century to design bus shelters that were in keeping with country villages. They are not only worth preserving in themselves; a watchful eye needs to be kept to ensure that some other piece of street furniture—say one of the new all-glass telephone boxes—is not crudely juxtaposed beside them.

STREET FURNITURE

An active local society needs to be in constant contact with not only the local authority but all the public utilities. The need is not only to retain what is worthwhile of the old, but also to ensure the new is sympathetic. This goes for signposts, lampposts, street nameplates and bollards.

The other key area to watch is property boundaries in the form of railings, fences, balustrades and walls. Untold damage was done, alas, to the look of older streets all over the country by the removal of iron railings. This was in fact a propaganda exercise to bring home to the men in the street the looming realities of total war: cast iron was not of any use in manufacturing guns or tanks. Railings survive where a hazard would have been created by their removal—for example, beside steps or around basement areas—but Victorian houses, which often had front gardens, suffered badly. Street frontages that were once elegant and harmonious have become ragged and disjointed with a different replacement wall or balustrade to every house. Old photographs, however, often exist showing the original railings. English Heritage, and some local authorities, may be willing to grant aid for the making of replacement railings.

Larger Victorian stuccoed houses often had balustrades rather than railings and in many cities these are at risk from the creation of hard parking stands in front of houses. The creation of a private parking space in front of a house often results in the loss of a parking space on the street, so there is no net gain; and a hazard for pedestrians is created.

Street furniture, though constantly under threat, is a source of fascination, and any literature or lecture on the subject is likely to attract attention. The watchword must be 'awareness'. If this can be created and kept constantly alive, streets will retain a great deal of interest for years to come.

⑫ MARKETS

MARKETS ARE ONE of the oldest features of town life. Numerous English towns were granted royal charters to hold weekly markets in the Middle Ages. Many continue the tradition of a market day; others established permanent, covered markets in the last century.

Today, with competition first from high street supermarkets and now from out of town hypermarkets, they are an endangered species. Yet open markets still command intense loyalty. In Chesterfield, a plan by the city council to build over the market place and incorporate it in a new, covered shopping precinct was opposed by a petition with more than 80,000 signatures, and the plans were withdrawn.

While street markets can easily adapt to changing demand from fresh vegetables to bric-a-brac, covered markets can present a greater problem.

In central London, the authorities initially planned to demolish both the Covent Garden Flower Market and Billingsgate Fish Market when the traders moved to new premises. Currently, the same approach has been adopted by the City Corporation and Tower Hamlets over Spitalfields Market.

Yet market buildings, even when they are quite plain, are usually attractive features of a town. Any substantial town or city faced with competition from out of town shopping needs to ensure its historic centre is a pleasant and welcoming place for people to come and shop and browse; and a lively, colourful market forms a natural focal point.

Where there is no call for a continued food market, market buildings have proved highly adaptable.

The main aim must be to find a public use providing public access. In commercial terms, this means shopping. As many market buildings stand in squares or have public space around them, they provide a natural place for people to congregate.

A well converted market building can inject new life into a whole area: Covent Garden is the classic example, where all the former premises of

MARKETS

Leeds Market. A thriving Northern market saved from redevelopment for today's traders and shoppers

fruit and vegetable wholesalers around the market have been taken over as shops, wine bars and restaurants. The emphasis should be on quite small units—for both retail and restaurant use. In this way, the market areas will be in strong contrast to local supermarkets and covered shopping centres, where large chain stores tend to congregate. Numerous former corn exchanges have been converted into shopping arcades accordingly.

Another obvious public use is as a museum. Manchester's former flower market, the Lower Campfield Hall, now houses the air and space gallery of the city's Science Museum, the high roofs providing ample space for large exhibits. Nearby, the city's former Cotton Exchange has become host to a space-age theatre, housed in an ingenious freestanding capsule constructed within the vast, empty dealing floor.

The key is to recognize that a market is a natural focal point of any town or city and therefore a potential asset. Even when market buildings are plain fare in architectural terms, simple cleaning and bright, fresh paint can quickly make them attractive and eyecatching; and they offer just the type of premises that appeal to many young and growing businesses. New, covered shopping centres—for all their obvious advantages in a climate such as ours—tend to be aimed at established shops with a brand name, which can pay a good rent. Converted markets can offer a different facility that adds a new dimension to urban life.

SAVE ACTION GUIDE

Case History
JUBILEE HALL, COVENT GARDEN, LONDON

THE SECRETARY OF State for the Environment has a duty—not just a power—laid on him by Parliament, to compile lists of buildings which are of historic and architectural interest. Self-evidently he does not go out and list them himself, and very early on historic building investigators were

Jubilee Hall, Covent Garden, London. Listed by the Department of the Environment under pressure from SAVE

appointed to carry out the task and guidelines for listing drawn up. But from time to time there have been cases where ministers, or more often officials, decide that listing is undesirable for what are, frankly, purely political grounds. Most of these cases come in the 'don't let's inconvenience our friends' category; and there are many instances where buildings, about to be sold by local authorities, nationalized industries or government departments, have escaped listing.

Quite apart from the injustice of adopting one policy for the public sector and another for the private, such tactics have often proved counterproductive and created more battles and delays, ultimately making sites more difficult to sell.

In such cases, the historic buildings inspector has usually recommended listing but has been overriden. Obviously, all ministers must have reasonable discretion in such matters, but if they depart from a clear, professional recommendation they must have good reason.

The Jubilee Hall in Covent Garden grew to be one such case. This was the original foreign flower market, one of a series of Victorian and Edwardian market buildings which give Covent Garden much of its character. The Greater London Council had determined to demolish it, and were hoping to obtain £1.5 million for the site. Successive requests for its listing had been rejected. The breakthrough came in 1980, when we received a copy of a letter to Michael Heseltine from a former Labour minister who had been responsible for historic buildings under the previous government. He wrote that the inspector had recommended the building for listing but the Greater London Council had convinced him and his colleagues that there was no alternative use and that listing would result in a 'very heavy loss of public funds'. SAVE, working with the Jubilee Hall campaign, had drawn up a scheme for alternative use, which involved building on the adjacent empty site. This, we contended, could provide a financial return comparable to that from a new building.

On the basis of Mr Freeson's letter, SAVE's solicitors advised that SAVE should take out an action for *mandamus*, a court order to force a minister to do what he is obliged to do under statute. A solicitor's letter was sent and within twenty-four hours the building was listed.

Case History
BILLINGSGATE FISH MARKET, LONDON

THE CITY CORPORATION was incensed at the listing of Billingsgate Fish Market in 1980. Yet in the end it sold the site for three times the amount that the City expected to obtain by demolishing the buildings.

When SAVE heard Sir Horace Jones' Victorian market was to close and the traders move to new premises in Docklands, we immediately contacted Richard Rogers, who had just received planning permission for the new Lloyd's building, to ask if he would work on a refurbishment scheme.

Billingsgate Fish Market, London. A major SAVE campaign ensured the preservation and imaginative conversion of the market

The old fish market, it was said, would sink into the Thames mud as soon as the cold store in the basement began to defrost. Even more colourful was the statement in the City Corporation's Annual Report that it had to be demolished 'due to corrosion by fish juices'.

SAVE's immediate task was to show that a conservation scheme could generate as healthy a financial return as a cleared site. The empty lorry-park to the west of the market provided the opportunity. The City Corporation had specified a maximum plot ratio of five to one across the whole site (that is, the equivalent of five storeys). SAVE's proposal was to transfer the 'air rights' of the old building on to the lorry-park site. The Corporation, in any event, envisaged a higher building on the lorry-park site to match the larger building beyond, with the silhouette stepped down to the level of the Georgian Custom House on the east side.

Working with Alan Stanton in Richard Rogers' office and the surveyor Hugh Cantlie, we did detailed calculations showing that good modern office floor space could be created. The old building, we proposed, should be adapted to create a mixture of shopping and fast food establishments, with restaurants and pubs in the corner pavilions on the river. Our belief was that this would not only be an attraction to City workers but a major facility for the millions of visitors to the Tower of London.

Various suggestions had been made that the market might be used as a commodity trading floor, but careful research persuaded us (correctly, as it transpired) that the brokers did not require a large open trading floor like the Stock Exchange or Lloyd's.

MARKETS

Following publication of SAVE's report, Michael Heseltine listed the building, and the City Corporation reacted immediately by applying for consent to demolish. Preservation, it was claimed, had not only jeopardized the market's move to Docklands but even the survival of the fishing industry of Great Britain! But tempers cooled and after some months the City Corporation decided to sell the building on the basis of a planning brief almost identical to SAVE's proposals.

We now determined to try to pursue our own scheme and teamed up with Trevor Osborne of Speyhawk. When the sealed bids were finally opened, Speyhawk turned out to be the underbidder—by just £2 million below the £24 million bid by the London and Edinburgh Trust.

First, the London and Edinburgh Trust built the new building on the lorry-park, constructed in blue glass like a giant cascade. Then they sold the old market to Citicorp which set about restoring it as a trading floor, aimed at meeting the demand generated by Big Bang. When they commissioned Richard Rogers as their architect, the wheel had come almost full circle.

The old fish market has been restored to an immaculate standard. All the ugly sheds along the riverfront have been removed and the newly cleaned oatmeal brickwork and fish-scale roofs, complete with gilded dolphins, are seen to full advantage. Inside, Horace Jones' remarkable roof, with its complex pattern of flying and interlacing ribs, has been restored in its entirety, and the brick vaults below the market cleaned and opened up. Richard Rogers has adopted a high-tech approach, carefully distinguishing between the old work and the new. There is a space-age element in many of the new fittings, where the contrast highlights the fine craftsmanship of the Victorian work.

As we go to press, it is a disappointment that the building is still not occupied, as a result of the recession. But one lesson we have learnt is that patient determination is essential in all rescue operations and one should never be discouraged by temporary setbacks.

⑬ HOSPITALS AND ASYLUMS

FROM SIXTEENTH- AND seventeenth-century hospices to Georgian workhouses, Regency infirmaries and vast Victorian lunatic asylums, the National Health Service has inherited a wealth of historic buildings, many of them listed.

With the massive changes currently taking place in the National Health Service and the controversial Care in the Community programme for the treatment of the mentally ill, hundreds of hospitals and mental asylums are being closed and sold off.

In terms of medical as well as architectural history, these buildings are of enormous interest, but only recently have they begun to be recognized as buildings of some value.

One of the problems is the way hospitals have had to be adapted for modern medical practice—often in the quickest and cheapest manner. New wards and accommodation blocks, laboratories and car-parks have all but masked the original building, whilst within it spacious airy wards, huge staircase halls and corridors have been extensively partitioned and bear no resemblance to their original plan.

Another problem is the general feeling amongst Health Service employees and their property advisors that their listed buildings are liabilities rather than assets. The process of disposal once a hospital is redundant can be frustratingly slow and unimaginative. Sometimes the health authorities demolish the old buildings themselves and sell a cleared site for redevelopment; sometimes they put the existing hospital on the market—very often in a dilapidated state, due to a lengthy programme of closure with minimal maintenance of the buildings.

And yet most redundant hospitals offer unique and exciting opportunities for conversion and re-use. They are often sited in very desirable locations: mental hospitals, in particular, such as the former county asylums which sprung up after the Lunacy Act of 1847, are located on the outskirts of towns, in landscaped grounds thoughtfully planned for the patients' well-being.

HOSPITALS AND ASYLUMS

The buildings themselves, often paid for by local philanthropists, were commissioned from leading architects. Awe-inspiring in size and design, often with highly decorated interiors and fine chapels, they are far from being the forbidding and depressing places one might expect. They can, with imagination, be adapted to a whole range of uses—residential, retail, business—becoming whole communities within themselves.

The important thing from the start is to assess all the buildings on the site in terms of existing resources. Often, simply because there is so much there, a developer will demolish whole chunks of good, solid buildings and then want to build anew. Yet ironically, very often the hospitals provide a density of building on a particular site that would not be permitted by planners nowadays. This is what has happened at the New End Hospital in Hampstead, where the developer, by adopting a conservation scheme, has gained more space than by demolition and rebuilding.

In the past few years, a number of former hospitals that were doomed to demolition have been successfully converted. The Royal Infirmaries of Shrewsbury and Sheffield, both handsome and centrally located within the town, have been restored and are now complexes of shops, offices and flats. The Royal Victoria Patriotic Building in Wandsworth, having suffered dreadfully from a fire, was sold for just £1 and considered to have no possible use. Yet its conversion to studios, workshops, flats and a drama school has won it several awards. The building is now worth a million times its original sale price!

The Royal Victoria Patriotic Building, Wandsworth. Converted to various uses, the building is a landmark of South London

SAVE ACTION GUIDE

A continuing problem with hospital closure is when just parts—and often the most architecturally interesting and attractive ones—of a hospital are closed due to cut-backs. But instead of leaving them shut up and prey to vandals and arson, they can be sold off separately and, of course, realize much-needed capital for the health authority. Even though the main hospital is to continue in use, as long as there is road access to the disused buildings and the local planning authority is flexible about change of use, then the buildings can have a future once more.

An example of this is the former workhouse at West Hill Hospital in Dartford, Kent. The health authority wished to demolish this very attractive group of buildings dating from 1838 to make way for a car-park. Left empty and decaying for some years, the buildings were at last put up for sale. Very soon they were acquired by a developer and are now being marketed as individual office units.

Case History
NEW END HOSPITAL, HAMPSTEAD, NORTH LONDON

A GROUP OF attractive and historic buildings in a commanding position in the heart of Hampstead conservation area came under threat in 1986. The earliest building is a mid-nineteenth-century workhouse and the most fascinating is the rotunda ward block, built in 1885. The circular plan was derived from the hospital tents of the Crimea, where improved ventilation helped reduce the risk of cross-infection. This building, along with two other structures, was listed, but others on the site, despite being equally attractive, had only conservation area protection.

When the hospital closed, the health authority, looking to capitalize as much as possible on this valuable site, wanted to sell the site for complete redevelopment. Camden Council required retention of the listed parts only, and, furthermore, would not agree to any offices on the site. This was a problem as some of the hospital buildings would readily convert to offices, but not so to flats.

In the face of a scheme which would have lost much of the old hospital, a local group determined to fight to save all the buildings and contacted SAVE for advice. At the time, we had just published *Hospitals: A Suitable Case for Treatment* and the New End looked to be a typical example of a wasted opportunity. Here were good and robust buildings, loved by local residents, which could be converted to a range of uses, but were to be demolished and replaced with mediocre high street architecture.

SAVE recommended that the local group draw up their own conservation scheme. On our advice, they contacted the architect, John Burrell, who showed how the buildings could be imaginatively adapted. A public inquiry was held and the conservation scheme won approval.

HOSPITALS AND ASYLUMS

Encouragingly, the developers agreed to adopt the Burrell scheme and this is now going ahead. They are happier now, for by conserving and converting the existing buildings they were able to achieve a higher percentage of floor space than if they had built anew. The conversion also shows how important it is for the planning authority to be flexible about change of use so the right scheme does not get blocked prematurely.

New End Hospital, Hampstead. The rotunda ward is to be incorporated into a conservation scheme for the whole site

⑭ INDUSTRIAL BUILDINGS

UNTIL RECENTLY, MOST industrial buildings were written off as hopeless white elephants. One furious developer responded as follows to SAVE's campaign to stop demolition of the great group of East India Company warehouses in Cutler Street, on the edge of the City of London: 'Your own pictures show that these are ghastly warehouses where only a few parts have any architectural merit—even Sing Sing and Alcatraz were better designed. I think you will make yourself a laughing stock if you ask people to help you save these frightful and ugly buildings.'

Now, however, it is recognized that great mills and warehouses have an austere grandeur entirely of their own and warehouses are so sought-after in London's docklands that many new blocks of apartments are built in warehouse style, with deeply recessed, arched windows and plain, unadorned brickwork.

The problem with industrial buildings is often their sheer size. A positive result of this, however, is that they are usually sturdily built; and their open-plan layouts make them highly adaptable to a range of uses, whether as offices, places of light industry or apartments.

The problems and potentials of these buildings are discussed and illustrated at length in SAVE's book, *Bright Future*. What is encouraging is that so many of them have been successfully recycled and are often occupied by the new electronics industries and other high-tech companies.

Large mills and warehouses none the less present the greatest challenges SAVE has had to face. Such buildings may often be derelict and vandalized, after years of minimal use and maintenance followed by total abandonment. Worse still, their surroundings may be in an appalling state, with rubble and wreckage strewn everywhere. The natural reaction is to clear the site and begin again.

For some time, the very deep plan—up to fifty or sixty feet from one outside wall to the other—appeared to make conversion difficult. But with the advent of the computer terminal, the need is often to reduce rather

INDUSTRIAL BUILDINGS

than increase the level of light in offices. Equally, with residential conversions, it may be feasible to put service cores, bathrooms and even kitchens in the centre of the building, with living rooms and bedrooms taking full advantage of existing windows.

Sometimes, it has been possible to open out light wells or atriums in the centre of the building and introduce more daylight in this way. In other cases, a whole section of a building has been scooped out in the centre, leaving only the two facades and thus creating an internal courtyard, which supplies light to the rest of the building.

As with many redundant buildings, the key to re-use may lie in the setting. Large industrial buildings may stand in a derelict wasteland that seems an irretrievable eyesore. But it is surprising how many stand near water—on a canal or river or by a millpond. Water, of course, was essential to drive steam machinery and any attractive building near water, once restored, tends to command a premium on the property market.

People are also constantly on the look out for buildings with character. It is often assumed that all potential purchasers and tenants are simply looking for flexible, functional floor space. This may be what they say. But again and again it is the buildings, or parts of buildings, with character, that prove to be the most sought after: an office of an unusual shape, a living room with a bay window.

Large mills and warehouses have been successfully adapted to virtually every kind of use—as museums, offices, shopping centres and flats. Some of the most successful conversions have been as start-up premises for new businesses providing floor space on an 'easy come, easy go' basis. The most ambitious and successful venture of this kind to date is Ernest Hall's rescue of the vast redundant Crossley textile mill, Dean Clough, at Halifax in West Yorkshire.

Here was one and a half million square feet of empty floor space in mills rising to ten storeys, all packed into a very tight site—a prime candidate for demolition and replacement by single-storey corrugated tin sheds. But Ernest Hall has created a centre for small businesses, refurbishing a wing or even a floor at a time, and providing expertise and encouragement to people setting up their own businesses. More than 200 small firms are established at Dean Clough, employing some 1,500 people. Initial tenants operated on a very small scale, but such is the charisma of the place that substantial, well-established companies are now renting whole floors—insurance companies, VAT men and, most recently, the Halifax Building Society. The uniqueness and history of the building has clearly been a major attraction for tenants and Mr Hall likes to point out that the first thing the visitor encounters on entering is an art gallery.

Ernest Hall's former partner, Jonathan Silver, has embarked on a similar venture at the massive Salt's Mill at Saltaire, outside Bradford. He has created the first David Hockney Gallery in Britain as well as attracting major companies to the office space.

SAVE ACTION GUIDE

Salt's Mill, Saltaire, West Yorkshire. A vast mill complex outside Bradford, it is to be used for a variety of purposes

The recognition that the industrial heritage of this country is as important as, say, our country houses and historic churches, has been affirmed in the Government's latest White Paper on the Environment, in which SAVE gets a mention:

> In recent years many private individuals and trusts have committed their efforts and enthusiasm to preserving some of the surviving remains of the industrial revolution, and to getting them back into working order. SAVE Britain's Heritage's recent book, *Bright Future*, illustrates what has been achieved—and the opportunities that still remain for conserving industrial buildings.

Satanic Mills

Few SAVE campaigns have struck as strong a chord as 'Satanic Mills'. Within ten days of the exhibition opening, we had entirely sold out of the companion volume, largely as a result of direct orders from people living in Lancashire and Yorkshire mill towns.

A book of this kind—one which was full of enthusiasm—had never been published.

The mills were a part of people's lives. They were fascinated by their history and did not want to see them disappear. Far from being unacceptable reminders of desperate working conditions, exploitation and poverty, people wanted to see them remain.

SAVE's exhibition was prompted by Randolph Langenbach, an American photographer who felt passionately that textile mills were an essential part

INDUSTRIAL BUILDINGS

of the life and landscape of the Pennines. He used to show photographs of Stoke-on-Trent just after the war, when the five pottery towns were crowded with more than 2,000 bottle kilns, creating a townscape without parallel anywhere. Thirty years later, just fifty remained. Stoke had lost its identity. From being a town unique in the world, it had become just like any other.

We had feared that attempts to claim 'satanic mills' were part of our heritage would simply be greeted with ridicule. Popular reaction changed all this and, not long after, Bradford became the first Northern town to promote its industrial heritage as a tourist attraction.

Weekend breaks were advertised in the national press and the visitor was given an official welcome as he got off the train. 'I've wanted all my life to see these great chimneys and mills', said the man from Kent. 'Tut lad', replied the Mayor—evidently not properly briefed—'We've knocked the lot down'.

But Bradford and Leeds both now have industrial museums, and SAVE went on to produce an illustrated mill trail—the first publication of its kind but supplying an obvious demand.

In addition, numerous mills have been listed by the Department of the Environment over the past ten years.

The key issue, of course, is what to do with the mills when they become redundant. Part of the problem is the sheer number involved. Visually, the richness of the landscape depends on preserving not just one or two mills but often a whole series, which are seen to dramatic effect only in sequence.

During the first great round of mill closures, many mills had found alternative industrial uses, and in Lancashire quite a number had been taken over by mail order businesses. But now there was much less industrial demand and, equally, much greater provision for modern purpose-built industrial units nearby.

For inspiration, we looked to North America, particularly Massachusetts, where in towns such as Lowell there were mills larger than the largest textile mill in Lancashire. Congress had recently voted $40 million to create America's first National Industrial Park—the urban counterpart of great scenic National Parks such as Yosemite.

Within a few years the derelict centre of Lowell had been spectacularly improved. Mills were converted for a wide range of uses, both commercial and residential—as centres for small businesses, as apartments, as shopping malls and as exhibition centres.

It was not long before local authorities in the North of England became interested in this potential and soon bevies of town councillors were flying across to New England to look at what was happening. Within less than ten years, the perception of historic mills has radically changed. Entrepreneurs, building preservation trusts and housing associations have all become involved.

SAVE ACTION GUIDE

Robinwood Mill, Todmorden, Lancashire. This outstanding nineteenth-century textile mill was to be demolished but is now looking for a new use

Case History
BRYNMAWR RUBBER FACTORY, GWENT, SOUTH WALES

FOR THOSE WHO might normally associate SAVE with country houses, Regency terraces and Victorian churches, the battle to save the former Dunlop Rubber Factory at Brynmawr in Gwent, South Wales, came as something of an eye-opener, proving that a building's historic significance is not tied purely to its age.

For buildings of a more recent date it has always been harder to drum up public support and, the day we went to visit Brynmawr in the pouring rain, the sight of stained and cracking concrete, rusting joists and broken glass was hardly inspiring!

Nevertheless, there was no doubt that this complex of factory buildings and boiler house, set beside a man-made lake, was a unique and remarkable example of post-war building; indeed, it had been listed grade II* by the Welsh Office a few months earlier. Built in 1946–52 by the Architects' Co-operative Partnership, of particular interest was its innovative use of concrete to form massive curved canopies with circular roof lights.

The factory was built to provide employment in the valleys, but it had been empty and disused since Dunlop moved out. It was seen by a local

INDUSTRIAL BUILDINGS

community still dogged by unemployment as an eyesore and an obstruction to a new development that could provide jobs.

Following a public inquiry a year before, the Secretary of State had refused demolition consent.

SAVE felt the local authority needed as much help as possible to find a solution for this building they openly despised.

We persuaded them to hold a one-day seminar to discuss the building and possible options for it. The meeting was chaired, at our suggestion, by Dame Margaret Weston, former Director of the Science Museum. At the end of the day we had managed to convince some—if not all—of the Blaenau Gwent councillors that the Rubber Factory was a building of immense interest and that an imaginative scheme of re-use could be of real benefit to the borough.

SAVE continued to sit on a working party for two years seeking a solution for the building and at last, in September 1990, a satisfactory scheme of conversion into industrial units, with housing around the lake, was presented.

It is hoped that this will now go ahead and, restored and repaired, Brynmawr will receive recognition as a modern masterpiece.

Case History
RODBORO BUILDINGS, GUILDFORD, SURREY

AT TIMES, IT is still difficult to persuade people of the merits of an industrial building, especially when it is large, semi-derelict and in poor repair.

Even though it may be of great architectural or historic significance, it will not be of pretty golden stone, half-timbered or thatched—the sort of historic building that has immediate aesthetic appeal—so it will fail to attract widespread support.

We came up against this problem with Rodboro Buildings in Guildford, Surrey.

Dating from 1900, they were constructed as the earliest purpose-built car factory in the world, and their listing reflected their significant historical importance. However, this was not understood by the borough council, which proposed demolishing them for traffic improvements. One councillor, describing the buildings as 'ugly, boring and without interest', argued that 'turning Rodboro Buildings into a second rate office block would give everybody the worst of all worlds.' Fortunately, many local people disagreed strongly. Like SAVE, they felt the buildings had enormous potential for re-use. Letters from SAVE were circulated to members of the council, and one year later the council has had an absolute volte-face, resolving to refurbish the buildings and rethink the appalling traffic scheme.

SAVE ACTION GUIDE

Case History
BATTERSEA POWER STATION, LONDON

FROM THE START, SAVE dubbed Battersea Power Station 'the Mount Everest of Preservaton'. The building is vast: one presumes that the main interior space must be in the area enclosed by the four massive chimneys. In fact, the two 500-feet long turbine halls are below on either side.

Battersea Power Station, standing on the Thames beside Chelsea Bridge, is unquestionably one of London's major landmarks. SAVE has never claimed it to be beautiful but rather sublime, in the eighteenth-century sense of being vast, imposing and awe-inspiring. One of the best views is of the north front, floodlit at night, seen from across the river.

What is not immediately clear is that the power station was built in two stages and throughout the Second World War it was only half the building it is today. The 1930s 'A' Station has the remarkable turbine hall lined with giant pillars, like two Hoover factories face to face. This was entirely clad in glazed tilework with stylish Art Deco detailing. The matching half was only completed in the 1950s, with a turbine hall in a simpler, modern style.

SAVE's immediate task was twofold: to rally public opinion and to show there was a possible alternative use. By the time SAVE gained access, all the magnificent machinery in the turbine hall was being stripped out. Initially, the Central Electricity Generating Board had resisted our

Battersea Power Station, London, has a reputation as The Mount Everest of Preservation'

INDUSTRIAL BUILDINGS

overtures, and it was only when we wrote direct to Tony Benn, then Secretary of State for Energy, that all doors magically opened.

Despite the inevitable jibes ('like an upturned billiards table', for example) the power station proved to have remarkable popular support. 'Londoners Love Battersea Power Station' was the conclusion of both *The Times* and the *Evening Standard* when they canvassed their readers' views about its demolition.

With the architect Martin Richardson, SAVE worked out a detailed scheme. Our initial problem was that we had no plans. The Central Electricity Generating Board professed to have none and making measured drawings was an impossibility given the scale of the building. Fortunately, Martin Richardson found a complete set, attached to the original planning application, in the archives of the old London County Council.

Given the vast amount of floor space, we decided to settle on a mixture of uses, with a major indoor sports arena in the huge area between the four chimneys. This consisted of an athletics track surrounded by raked seating. Used as a championship tennis court, the seating capacity could be considerably extended.

Our publication was received with some scepticism by the Electricity Board. 'You have produced this at a very awkward time for us', we were told by the Deputy Director, who was struggling with the Unions over the loss of jobs stemming from closure. But one lesson SAVE has learnt is that it is never too soon to start thinking about the future of an endangered historic building.

Martin Richardson was determined to follow through our initial efforts and established that the Borough of Wandsworth would welcome the opportunity to consider an application for change of use. In 1982, SAVE became the proud recipient of planning permission for conversion of the power station for leisure and recreational purposes.

Battersea Power Station had been listed in 1980 by Michael Heseltine, one of his first batch of interwar listings, drawn up in response to campaigning by SAVE and the Thirties Society for protection of buildings from the 1920s and 1930s.

The Electricity Board decided therefore a serious attempt must be made to market the buildings and invited architect-developer teams to tender. While there would undoubtedly be no lack of amazing proposals, their need was understandably to identify one with a substantial degree of financial backing.

SAVE was naturally approached by a number of developers: one wanted to turn the power station into a giant version of the Paris Lido, with 2,000 diners watching a spectacular floorshow; others envisaged hotels and offices. In the end, there appeared to be only two serious contenders: first a rubbish incineration scheme that would have perpetuated the industrial use of the building and ensured the chimneys continued to smoke. This would have saved the building, but involved the construction of a vast elevated road inside the Art Deco turbine hall above the bases of the pillars to gain sufficient tipping height for the rubbish.

The other scheme was the proposal to turn the power station into a vast Disney-style indoor entertainment centre. This was initially put forward by a consortium led by Sir David Roche. The Roche team were the winners but, soon after, in swashbuckling style, the consortium was taken over by one of the partners, John Broome, who managed the highly successful Alton Towers leisure park in Staffordshire.

Spectacular plans were drawn up with the help of American consultants for sensational rides but, subsequently, it has been the power station itself which has had the rough ride. The work of decommissioning, especially asbestos removal, proved far more difficult than was envisaged and the project ground to a halt while attempts were made to refinance the scheme. The latest position is that John Broome has raised £70 million from the sale of Alton Towers and obtained planning permission for substantial development on the land he acquired next to the power station from British Rail. Now he is seeking to organize a development scheme that will enable him to proceed with the conversion of the power station as originally planned.

This, in SAVE's view, is the use which will allow the maximum number of people to enjoy spectacular architectural interiors at close quarters. But if for any reason it does not proceed, the refuse disposal group have been expressing interest again. Battersea Power Station remains unscaled, the Mount Everest of preservation; but fortunately, there remain people determined to make the ascent.

⑮ RAILWAY STATIONS AND STRUCTURES

DURING THE 1960S and 1970s, the Beeching axe condemned dozens of fine stations to closure and demolition. But following SAVE's exhibition, 'Off the Rails', mounted in 1977 at the Heinz Gallery in the Royal Institute of British Architects, British Rail's attitude towards historic buildings has, thankfully, changed quite markedly.

Off the Rails

The exhibition attacked British Rail's record in maintaining its historic buildings. British Rail, we said in the catalogue, had gone off the rails in failing to appreciate the grandeur of its architectural heritage:

> Britain invented the railway, pioneered its application to passenger travel and built the most extensive network of lines anywhere in the world. Yet this unparalleled legacy of stations, hotels, train sheds, bridges, viaducts and signal boxes is being steadily dissipated. Line after line has been axed, and hundreds of buildings have been left to fall into decay inviting vandalism . . .

The exhibition was a substantial polemic by any standards, but British Rail at that moment had a new chairman, Peter Parker, who came to the exhibition and invited us to a debate in his office on the issues. While robustly defending British Rail's position, he undertook to look at ways in which more consideration could be given to restoring historic buildings and finding new uses for them.

The result over the next ten years was to be a major turnaround in the attitudes of both British Rail and the British Rail Property Board. British Rail's Environment Panel was reconstituted, with Simon Jenkins (who had been appointed a member of the main British Rail board) later becoming its chairman. In 1985, British Rail established a new Railway Heritage Trust with a fund of nearly £1 million to give in grants for the repair of listed railway structures in operational use. This has risen to £1,290,000 for 1990–91.

SAVE ACTION GUIDE

As British Rail is under constant pressure to make economies and increase profitability, the existence of a top-up fund for restoration projects has prompted the repair and improvement of numerous station buildings which might otherwise have been left to decay slowly or actually been demolished.

Railway Heritage Trust-aided projects have included the cleaning and repair of the towers of Cannon Street Station on the Thames, in London; the rebuilding of the delightful station of Great Malvern, in Worcestershire; and the repair of the remarkable viaduct on the line to Mallaig, in Western Scotland, in its time the largest concrete structure in the world.

In repeated cases the Railway Heritage Trust has successfully helped to negotiate additional grants from other sources—including district and county councils—with the result that British Rail's investment in the trust is often multiplied in value two or three times.

Most important of all is the related recognition by many members of British Rail's management that clean, attractive historic stations have a positive appeal for the customer and can be just as much of an asset as wholly new stations in many circumstances. And, of course, the cost of straightforward cleaning and painting can be substantially less than in the case of a new building.

British Rail's problem is that financial pressures lead to constant cuts in staff, and more and more stations are de-manned. In such cases, it is desirable that stations, or parts of them, are leased as soon as possible. British Rail has learnt from experience that it can be dangerous to sell the freehold of a building if the station is still in use. Also, too often the new owner has bought the building with no realistic plans for it and, while treating the building as a maturing antique, has left it exposed to the weather.

The best solution is for British Rail and other owners to offer a long lease with a repairing clause ensuring that the building is properly maintained and repaired. In many cases, if it is left to rot, British Rail takes the blame even it if no longer owns the station.

A parallel fund to the Railway Heritage Trust has been created for redundant structures under which the Property Board will, in appropriate cases, contribute a sum equivalent to the cost of demolishing the structure to any organization that takes over responsibility for its restoration.

This has transformed the outlook for structures such as viaducts. The prospect of finding uses for redundant viaducts had looked exceedingly slim, but recently a series of potential uses and users have come forward. The Sustrans Trust has been able to acquire a number of important viaducts as part of the long-distance footpath and cycle ways it specializes in creating. A specially formed trust has taken over the spectacular listed Smardale Gill in Cumbria. Most interesting of all is the proposal by Stephen Weeks to acquire a series of viaducts and introduce holiday trains converted into railway cottages.

RAILWAY STATIONS AND STRUCTURES

Case History
LANGLEY STATION, SLOUGH, BERKSHIRE

THIS DELIGHTFUL CHÂTEAU-STYLE station came under imminent threat of demolition in 1986. British Rail had decided to close the ticket office and no longer required the building. Prompt action by SAVE secured its listing, and the restoration of the building was supported by grants from the Railway Heritage Trust.

Langley Station, Slough, Berkshire. Saved by spotlisting

⑯ PUBS AND HOTELS

IN NUMEROUS DISMAL council housing estates, the one building of character to survive is the pub. Many Victorian pubs have, or did have, exceptionally fine interiors, with a succession of different bars, with richly engraved or stained glass, as well as colourful glazed tiles and a wealth of carved and turned woodwork.

The problem with pubs is the constant pressure for change and improvement. Small bars are thrown together and enlarged, seating and counters are changed, restaurants and discos are introduced. Very often this work is done not by architects, but by designers, decorators and shopfitters. Little consideration may be given to original or historic fittings and fixtures. Yet the irony is that the aim is often to create a 'heritage' look, complete with padded seats, cast-iron tables and gaslights. But unfortunately the real thing has been replaced by a pale imitation.

Part of the problem is that pub interiors have been relatively little recorded or studied and any local society or group producing a leaflet on a town's pubs and hostelries is doing a service. Certainly, it is worth combing the local library and local newspapers for old photographs; and check whether the pub has listed building protection.

The value of pubs that are all of a piece is self-evident. More complex are those such as the coaching inns, which still exist in many county towns and which tend to contain a wealth of woodwork and panelling of different dates. Very often the later work may not be as good as the original, even if it was matched up with some care, and the whole interior may be dismissed as 'boiled' or fake. Precisely this happened at The George Inn in Southwark, the one London coaching inn to survive today. The National Trust, which owns The George, though retaining the Victorian bar parlour, took a purist line elsewhere and was not prepared to defend the matching later work that the brewers wished to remove in order to enlarge the restaurant area. The essential principle, however, is to recognize that later alterations very often add to a building's historical interest.

PUBS AND HOTELS

A much closer inspection needs to be made of the numerous pubs and roadhouses built in the 1920s and 1930s. Great care was often taken in fitting out their interiors.

A new threat faces the traditional country pub. Many of these are very simple buildings, hardly distinguishable from neighbouring cottages; and this is the problem. If they come on the market, they will fetch more as houses than as pubs. Yet, as village shops, schools and churches close, the pub may be the sole surviving place where a community can gather. Continued use as a pub is far more likely to preserve the building's integrity. Indeed, conversion into a house could be said to eradicate its essential character; and, of course, any such change to a listed building would require consent.

The hotel industry is at a critical point. For years, the emphasis has been on creating new, modern hotels, yet it is apparent that increasing numbers of people recoil from the standardized, bland uniformity of chain hotels and seek individuality and character. In the United States, following the Tax Reform Act of 1976, which provided incentives to restore and re-use large buildings, numerous grand Victorian and early twentieth-century hotels have been immaculately restored. Original paint schemes have been copied, carpets rewoven, chandeliers rehung or remade, and period furniture reintroduced. In Britain, it is the country house hotel that has substantially met this demand for quality and history, but the opportunity exists to revamp or revive many purpose-built hotels, particularly in

Bembridge Royal Spithead Hotel, Isle of Wight. A seaside hotel demolished in spite of SAVE's efforts to keep it standing

resorts and seaside towns. This may be a slow process. The important point is to ensure the buildings do not disappear in the meantime. Many have enjoyed a desultory existence for some years as rented or furnished apartments and now, thanks to their prominent positions with good views, they may be seen to be ripe for redevelopment as prestige apartments. They may look forlorn today, largely because they have lost many of their ornamental features, but fresh paint and the reinstatement of bargeboards, shutters and balconies can transform them.

Case History
THE GEORGE INN, NAILSWORTH, GLOUCESTERSHIRE

AN SOS CALL to SAVE brought the news that workmen were on the roof stripping the stone tiles off this early nineteenth-century coaching inn. Though it was not listed, it was clearly an essential and much-loved part of the village. Massed local protest and a twenty-four-hour guard prompted the council to act: at SAVE's suggestion, they designated a conservation area around the building. This was done at a special council meeting two days later and the demolition contractors called off.

⑰ THEATRES, CINEMAS AND PUBLIC BUILDINGS

A FEW YEARS ago, cinemas and even theatres looked a doomed species, but now both are enjoying a remarkable revival.

In 1982 under SAVE's aegis, *Curtains!!! A New Life for Old Theatres* was published, cataloguing all known surviving and lost theatres. Following this, the Theatres Trust has been established and by Act of Parliament must be notified of any planning applications affecting theatres.

The research for *Curtains!!!* revealed that a remarkable number of theatre interiors, though long-closed and even abandoned, survived in almost unaltered condition all over the country. One by one, these have been purchased, restored and reopened by specially formed trusts and companies. Thanks to the work of the *Curtains!!!* group and the Theatres Trust, a pool of historical information, old photographs and specialist knowledge is readily available, and any proposal to restore a disused historic theatre will receive significant professional support and resources.

Actors and actresses have also begun to take an increasing interest in the preservation of theatres and the vigil mounted at the Rose Theatre in Southwark, when it was threatened with imminent destruction, marked an important turning point. The presence of well-known actors and actresses at a protest meeting, demonstration or sit-in is a guarantee of publicity, powerfully boosting the cause and bringing smiles to their agents' faces.

More and more interest is being taken in the history and architecture of cinemas, both in the pre-First World War incunabula and in the often stylish Moderne Odeons and Gaumonts. The most important point to recognize and investigate is that many 1920s and 1930s cinemas had fine interiors. Good Art Deco interiors abounded, but the most exciting were the 'atmospherics' auditoriums (stage sets in themselves, with exotic architecture or landscapes round the walls and a star-spangled sky above).

Many of these interiors have only survived through use as bingo halls but, now that cinema attendances are increasing, there is the prospect that they may come back into use. The essential problem is that most cinema operators want to create three or four small cinemas within the shell of the cinema and not one large auditorium with between 1,000 and 2,000 seats. What is essential in these circumstances is to ensure as far as possible that any subdivision is reversible and does the least amount of damage to original features. The trade-off for partition must be retention of original decoration, light fixtures, boxes, foyers and staircases.

Fortunately, a sympathetic form of subdivision is often the cheapest. For example, most interwar cinemas had an upper circle, either behind or above the stalls. This can be partitioned off as a separate cinema. Further, smaller cinemas can be created by dividing each level of seating into two. In this way, the original decoration on the flanking walls can be left undisturbed and even the original seating, if it is of merit, by simply removing a few seats on one side to create an extra aisle.

If your local cinema is under threat, it is important to assess its quality. Make a thorough inspection of the interior. Even if it is in a shabby or forlorn state, there will probably be photographs available showing how the reinstatement of lost detail—both inside and out—could quickly restore its original looks. Be sure to contact SAVE, the Thirties Society and the Cinemas & Theatres Association.

Case History
THE LYCEUM, LIVERPOOL

SAVE'S LONG CAMPAIGN for the Liverpool Lyceum shows that, however late the hour, however overwhelming the odds, no fine historic building is a lost cause until it is physically demolished. When we began our campaign in 1978, the Lyceum was already condemned. Consent had been given to demolish the grade I listed building and planning permission granted for a massive redevelopment on the site. Revoking the planning permission was likely to cost a substantial, six-figure sum.

The original consent had been granted because British Rail had successfully argued a case of overriding need for the site on part of a new inner railway loop. In the event, they had been unable to reach agreement with the developers and built the station next door.

Now that the underlying reason for demolition had vanished, a campaign began in Liverpool for its reprieve. It was one of the best grass-roots campaigns SAVE has been involved with. Local councillors and bigwigs were mercilessly lampooned (humour has always been one of Liverpool's strongest suits); and posters, leaflets, petitions, Lyceum badges and Lyceum cupcakes were all produced in thousands, owing to the inspiration of Florence Gerstein, a local teacher.

SAVE's contribution was to take up the issue at a national—indeed international—level. In Moscow, we collected 150 signatures for a telegram to the British Prime Minister from delegates at the Congress of the International Council on Monuments and Sites. We published a lightning

THEATRES, CINEMAS AND PUBLIC BUILDINGS

The Lyceum, Liverpool. A massive local and national campaign forced the Government to purchase the building, preventing its demolition

SAVE campaign leaflet quoting numerous golden opinions of the Lyceum's architect, Thomas Harrison of Chester. 'Harrison', his great contemporary, C. R. Cockerell, had written, 'has a spark divine.' Lord Elgin—of the Marbles—called him in 1835 'the most classical and scientific architect of his day'. Sir Nikolaus Pevsner described the Lyceum as 'one of the finest early buildings in Liverpool.'

The Lyceum had opened in 1802 as a combined library, newsroom and coffee room with 800 members. Externally it was chastely Grecian with a handsome recessed Ionic portico; inside, the library was housed in an attractive domed rotunda, and the newsroom had classical bas-reliefs anticipating those at the Travellers' Club in London by twenty-five years.

By June 1978, the Labour Environment Secretary, Peter Shore, had received such a barrage of protest that he had begun to think the unthinkable—revoking the planning permission and compensating the club.

However, negotiations took so long that, following the general election of April 1979, the final decision lay before a new Secretary of State, Michael Heseltine, who threw the future of the Lyceum into question again. 'My predecessor', he said, 'as an act of faith decided to purchase the club with the underlying implication that the state would then spend between £0.75 and £1.5 million on restoration works. At that point we would have an empty but beautiful early nineteenth-century building. We would not have a development that would create jobs, or stimulate economic activity, or make valuable use of an empty site.' Our campaign began anew: the new shopping centre could be built behind the club.

To our delight, Michael Heseltine finally confirmed the decision to purchase the club. The cost, including essential repair work, came to £635,000, but in 1984 the building was sold on to the Post Office for £320,000—so the cost to the taxpayer was far less than the £0.75–£1.5 million Heseltine had feared.

As so often, the underlying problem was not the decay of the building and the cost of restoring it, but planning conditions set upon the site. The planners had insisted that the proposed shopping centre across the road from the Lyceum should be serviced by an overhead road beginning on the Lyceum site. Building a ramp and bridge strong enough to take forty-ton lorries imposed a colossal financial penalty and meant demolition was inevitable for 'practical' reasons. However, on examination, the overhead road was not necessary and would be a visual blight on the street that it crossed. Once it was dispensed with, the figures became possible and, better still, the shopping centre has been built behind the attractive eighteenth- and nineteenth-century frontages on Bold Street.

Now came the long wait when it seemed that the Lyceum might never be restored. But in June 1990 we at last received an invitation to the formal opening of a new Central Liverpool Post Office in the restored Lyceum.

The newsroom now has smart, panelled counters like a branch of Coutts, and the rotunda has been restored as a philatelic centre selling a whole range of antique stamps, first-day covers and postal souvenirs.

Thus, the general public has direct access to the two main interiors of the club—an important point given the intense local feeling and campaigning to save the building. Every part of the building has been put to good use: the basement, opening out at pavement level on to Bold Street, has been let to a building society; the warren of accommodation on the roof has been converted to provide offices for forty post office executives, who beamed with delight at their new premises.

⑱ PUBLIC PARKS

FREDERICK LAW OLMSTED, designer of New York's famous Central Park, held that the touchstone of his long and illustrious career was his first visit to Birkenhead Park in Liverpool, one of a series of large, fine public parks in Northern towns laid out to provide fresh air and recreation in smog-ridden industrial towns. Today, Preston has the largest and best preserved of these.

The appeal of these parks lay in the fact that they were the work of the leading landscape designers of the day. Many had, and some still do have, a proud tradition of municipal gardening, as well as many mature specimen trees.

Over the years, many of these parks have become run down as public spending has been cut. Ornamental buildings and conservatories have often been allowed to decay or have even been demolished; fountains have ceased to play; lakes and ponds are choked with weeds or have lost their water; carefully planned vistas have been crowded out by saplings or shrubs; and dying trees have not been replaced.

And, of course, once any place becomes unkempt, it is not only an invitation to litter and vandalism, but is also seen as an opportunity for development. Yet almost always there is a group of committed local people who hold these parks in great affection and make regular use of them.

The need therefore is first to resist any unsuitable proposals for development. Public parks were for outdoor recreation: large, covered sporting areas—as have been proposed at Bournemouth—will completely change this character. The boundaries of a public park must be sacrosanct —once a slice is taken for road widening or for some community project, however worthy, a dangerous precedent has been set. Substantial buildings in parks invariably attract vehicles—cars, vans, even lorries—which are wholly unacceptable in an area set aside for young children to play in.

Old photographs, prints and newspaper cuttings can all provide fascinating clues as to the origins and early history of these parks, showing them in their prime, and how they could look if a systematic programme of reinstatement was introduced.

FUTURE AGENDA

Strengthening listing policies

In recent years, the Government has accelerated the listing programme with very welcome results. As SAVE pointed out in 1975, there were numerous seventeenth- and eighteenth-century buildings in country areas that were quite unprotected. As a result, the total of listed buildings increased from 227,155 in 1975 to 433,654 in 1989.

Today, nearly all buildings built before 1700, and most Georgian buildings that survive in anything like their original condition, are likely to be listed. The weaknesses lie with Victorian and later buildings. Until 1968 the cut-off date for listing was 1840. After that, a pilot attempt was made, with the help of the Victorian Society, to list the principal works of the principal Victorian architects—some twenty-five architects were included on the initial list.

While a much wider range of Victorian buildings are now listed, including many industrial buildings such as railway stations and textile mills, many good, unusual Victorian buildings remain unlisted. This is simply because the criteria used for listing Victorian buildings are more restrictive than those used for Georgian buildings. Yet the legacy of the nineteenth century was exceptionally rich—in both quality and quantity. We are now sufficiently far away from it to make an objective assessment of its architecture. The same criteria should apply to all Victorian—and indeed Edwardian—buildings as apply to Georgian ones.

SAVE was also instrumental in persuading Michael Heseltine to start systematic listing of buildings from the 1920s and 1930s. An initial selection of inter-war buildings—about 200 in all—had been made by Sir Nikolaus Pevsner, but these were almost entirely Modern Movement buildings. SAVE and the Thirties Society argued that the lists should cover all styles of the era—from neo-Georgian and neo-Tudor to Art Deco and Moderne. Pevsner had concentrated on the main works of the leading modern architects, but this era—like every era—also produced its own characteristic

FUTURE AGENDA

building types, such as public swimming baths (especially outdoor ones), road houses and cinemas.

The criteria laid down by Parliament for listing is that buildings must be of special architectural or historic interest. With buildings of the 1920s and 1930s, ministers had deemed that they must be of outstanding interest to be listed.

The word 'outstanding' has an exact connotation. It was introduced in the 1953 Act creating the three Historic Buildings Councils for England, Scotland and Wales and enabling them to make grants to buildings of outstanding interest. The intention was to restrict grants effectively to grade I and grade II* buildings, which represent two and four per cent of the total number of listed buildings respectively.

Restrictive listing of 1920s and 1930s architecture to outstanding buildings only has meant that a great many buildings of considerable quality remain unprotected. This is particularly serious as buildings are most vulnerable between fifty and a hundred years after they were built. Unless listing is made less restrictive, some towns could lose their best examples of 1920s and 1930s architecture.

With post-war architecture, listing is inevitably more selective still. To our delight, in 1988 William Waldegrave introduced what is known as the 'Thirty Year Rule', which had already been used in Scotland for many years. This means that buildings can be considered for listing after thirty years, and now, in very exceptional circumstances, buildings of outstanding quality will be listed after ten years.

The problem, however, is that the Government has refused to make any significant listings of post-1939 buildings. A draft list prepared by English Heritage was substantially rejected.

Ministers considered the list was a political bombshell—it included a number of buildings, such as high-rise housing blocks, which have become profoundly unpopular.

A similar argument developed over Erno Goldfinger's Alexander Fleming House, the Department of Health offices at Elephant and Castle. Was this a masterpiece of modern architecture or a 1960s monstrosity at its worst?

In any event, arguments against particular modern buildings should not be allowed to create a stalemate about modern buildings in general. Roehampton estate is among a handful of post-war projects which not only won international acclaim when they were built, but have always been held up outside Britain as the premier pieces of Modern Movement architecture this country has produced.

Conservation areas

The definition adopted by Wandsdyke District Council is admirably clear. It states that 'designation of a conservation area is a recognition by the planning authority that the area's established architectural and historic qualities are worthy of preservation and enhancement.'

Over 6,000 conservation areas have been designated and have been instrumental in safeguarding historic town centres from more of the comprehensive redevelopment that wrought such devastation in the 1960s and early 1970s.

SAVE's current concern was well illustrated by the inspector's report on the No. 1 Poultry appeal. Here, he asserted that 'the designation of conservation areas is not in my opinion intended as a means to secure the preservation of buildings that are not judged worth of statutory listing.'

Those who fought for the introduction of conservation areas thought exactly the opposite. Duncan Sandys, who introduced the Bill in Parliament in 1966, made the specific point that 'it is not enough merely to preserve isolated buildings.' The Department of the Environment circular 86/72, providing guidelines on the new legislation, made the case for conserving more modest buildings in the clearest terms:

> The demolition of even a single building, which may not be architecturally or historically significant in itself, and the construction of some new building in its place could result in the character or appearance of a conservation area, or part of it, being severely prejudiced. In such circumstances the whole purpose of designating the conservation area could be undermined.

A national trust for historic chapels

There are some buildings of such surpassing quality and completeness that they must be preserved intact. The National Trust has taken on numerous country houses with their collections and furniture to preserve them in their entirety. The Church of England has established the Redundant Churches Fund which operates, in effect, as a national trust for disused parish churches, with more than 200 outstanding churches in its care.

No such alternative exists for the churches of other denominations, however fine, not even for the Church of Scotland or the Church in Wales. For a time the Department of the Environment appeared willing to take a number of the early Nonconformist chapels into guardianship—but some time before English Heritage was established in 1984, clear resistance had developed to increasing the number of buildings in guardianship.

Yet the beauty and importance of many Nonconformist chapels is that they are all of a piece, with pews, galleries, pulpit, rostrum and organ all built in as fixtures. The best examples—some of the early ones being very small—need to be preserved, exactly as they are, for the nation.

The Redundant Churches Fund was set up initially as a partnership between Church and State, with the Church contributing two thirds of the budget on the basis that the Church has a continuing interest in these buildings. Since then the proportion of government aid has steadily increased, reaching seventy per cent in 1990. But the principle of partnership remains.

FUTURE AGENDA

By contrast, the other denominations have resolutely refused to contribute anything to a new fund for the preservation of the best of their redundant churches and chapels.

A way out of this impasse does, however, exist. When the Poll Tax was introduced the Churches Main Committee immediately made representations that the Churches should be exempt—on the basis that rates had never been charged on rectories or manses.

The Government, however, was unwilling to grant any general exemption for the clergy (with the exemption of certain contemplative orders). But as the Churches had said that paying Poll Tax would impair their ability to keep historic churches in repair, the Secretary of State offered by way of return a £3 million increase per annum in English Heritage church grants. Some of this money should be channelled on an annual basis into the creation of a chapels fund.

The cost of taking, say, half a dozen chapels into guardianship over two years need not be exorbitant. The repairs could be phased over a number of years. The sums involved would not be more than ten per cent of the extra money English Heritage has available for churches.

Protection of parks and gardens

The United Kingdom Government has failed seriously, consistently and conspicuously to provide adequate protection for historic parks and gardens. As a result, needless destruction and erosion is taking place on an increasing scale. The principal threats at present come from leisure proposals and from road building. Proposals for golf courses have particularly serious implications for landscape parks as they not only involve a fundamental change of character—from grazing to mown fairways, greens and tees—but invariably involve substantial building. This often results in not simply a clubhouse, but a major hotel complex, holiday houses and perhaps a conference centre, to enable the place to survive during the winter. Most of these applications, it should be added, are purely speculative. Once permission is granted, construction work does not begin, but the property is placed on the market at a much increased price.

For twenty years, a number of local planning authorities have designated important parks and gardens as conservation areas. This is an important step. It ensures a protected area is marked on all planning maps, sending out a signal to developers, statutory undertakers and highway authorities. It also—in theory at least—provides protection for trees, which can be particularly important where a country house park is in divided ownership and is being ploughed. Disgracefully, the Department of the Environment has consistently discouraged local authorities from providing this small measure of protection, though fortunately its advice has not always been heeded.

In addition, the 1983 National Heritage Act made provisions for Registers of Historic Parks and Gardens to be drawn up. In England, the register, compiled by English Heritage, now includes more than 1,200 properties. However, as inclusion on the register provides no statutory protection, damage continues.

When the proposal for the register was debated in Parliament, ministers gave undertakings that statutory protection was not on its way, to dispel fears that owners might be obliged to maintain their gardens to the point of being told what flowers they could grow.

There is no need for any such burden to be imposed on owners. What is required is an element of protection from outside threats such as road building. This, many owners would welcome.

No new legislation is needed: simply a change in the planning circulars, or one of the new planning policy guidelines, obliging planning authorities and government departments to pay special regard to the merits of properties on the register. This would be parallel to the special regard that planning authorities are obliged to give to proposals affecting conservation areas (under Section 277(8) of the 1971 Planning Act). It would thus bring the register within the existing framework of structural plans and planning applications.

English Heritage admits that, under the present system, many local authorities faced with planning applications affecting historic parks and gardens do not avail themselves of the specialist advice that English Heritage can provide. A second measure that has been suggested would be to require compulsory notification of such proposed developments by local authorities to, say, English Heritage and the Garden History Society, in the same way that applications to demolish or alter listed buildings have to be referred to specialist bodies such as the Georgian Group and the Victorian Society.

Repairs powers

One of SAVE's most consistent messages has been that local authorities must use the powers given them by Parliament to serve Repairs Notices on owners of decaying listed buildings, and in extreme cases to use their reserve powers to carry out emergency repairs on empty buildings themselves and send the bill to the owner.

There are, however, some very large or important buildings that local authorities feel are too big for them to take on. Here it is vital that the Secretary of State or English Heritage use their powers to serve Repairs Notices and set an example.

The serving of Repairs Notices achieves more than the repair or sale for restoration of individual buildings. It sends out a clear, unmistakable signal that the neglect of listed buildings will not be tolerated and decisions about their future have to be taken.

Once it is known that a local planning authority is willing to take action against the owners of buildings needing repair, the number of such buildings may reduce drastically.

FUTURE AGENDA

It is not simply lack of funds that leads to decay of listed buildings. Very often the owners have substantial resources but are hoping that the building will become so derelict that permission for a lucrative redevelopment will be granted.

In such cases, owners will be very wary of allowing their listed properties to decay to such an extent that the council can purchase them for a price reflecting their current condition.

Demonstration projects

The general principle behind allocating historic buildings grants is to spread the money as fairly and evenly as possible. But sometimes a higher percentage of grant concentrated on one pilot project can serve as a demonstration of what can be achieved and prove a highly effective way of encouraging others.

The Government set such a lead with the four Cathedral City studies in the 1960s—of Bath, Chester, Chichester and York—which laid down the conservation-oriented policies and plans that have been the key to their prosperity ever since.

Subsequently, SAVE has suggested to the Department of the Environment that a similar series of four to six studies should be initiated to encourage conservation efforts in other types of historic towns now suffering from economic decline—say, a spa, a seaside resort, a textile town and a mining town. In the United States, the $40 million invested in the decaying mill town of Lowell in Massachusetts has not only transformed the fortunes of Lowell but also stimulated interest and activity in mill towns nearby.

SAVE placed particular emphasis on Halifax in a series of reports, beginning with *The Concrete Jerusalem* in 1976 and continuing with *Halifax: Buildings at Risk* in 1983. Stimulated by the Prince of Wales' plea for the town and the involvement of Business in the Community under his aegis, Halifax's prospects have been transformed. SAVE believes similar initiatives should be launched for other towns. Once Halifax was seen to be benefiting from a positive approach to conservation, other nearby mill towns such as Burnley and Huddersfield sought to follow.

For years, the English seaside resorts have been in decline, as holiday makers have been lured to the Mediterranean. At last there are signs of a revival. The question is whether this revival simply brings more damaging development and disfigurement, or genuinely improves the looks and attractiveness of these resorts.

In many seaside towns, the most attractive residential streets are wholly unprotected by either listing or conservation area designation. By concentrating effort in one seaside town, such as, say, Morecambe in Lancashire, the whole appearance of the town could be transformed. Seaside towns tend to be colourful places: quite simple town schemes concentrating on repairs and painting of elevations, removal of ugly signs and alterations could have startling results.

SAVE ACTION GUIDE

APPENDIX I
WHAT LISTING MEANS

Extract from Department of the Environment Circular 8/87, 25 March 1987: Historic Buildings and Conservation Areas—Policy and Procedures

How the Buildings Are Chosen

The principles of selection for the lists were drawn up by the Historic Buildings Council (the functions of the former Historic Buildings Council for England are now carried out by the Historic Buildings and Monuments Commission (HBMC)) and approved by the Secretary of State. They cover four groups:

All buildings built before 1700 which survive in anything like their original condition are listed.

Most buildings of 1700–1840 are listed, though selection is necessary.

Between 1840 and 1914 only buildings of definite quality and character are listed, and the selection is designed to include the principal works of the principal architects.

Between 1914 and 1939, selected buildings of high quality are listed.

After 1939, a few outstanding buildings are listed.

In choosing buildings, particular attention is paid to:

Special value within certain types, either for architectural or plannng reasons or as illustrating social and economic history (for instance, industrial buildings, railway stations, schools, hospitals, theatres, town halls, markets, exchanges, almshouses, prisons, lock-ups, mills).

Technological innovation or virtuosity (for example, cast iron, prefabrication, or the early use of concrete).

Association with well-known characters or events.

Group value, especially as examples of town planning (for example, squares, terraces or model villages).

Grading

The buildings are classified in grades to show their relative importance as follows:

Grade I These are buildings of exceptional interest (only about two per cent of listed buildings so far are in this grade).

Grade II* These are particularly important buildings of more than special interest (some four per cent of listed buildings).

Grade II These are buildings of special interest, which warrant every effort being made to preserve them.

Grade III A non-statutory and now obsolete grade. Grade III buildings are those which, whilst not qualifying for the statutory list, were considered nevertheless to be of some merit.

APPENDIX II
SAVE PUBLICATIONS

SAVE has published over ninety reports. A full list can be obtained from their offices, whilst a selection is listed below.

SAVE REPORT: HERITAGE YEAR TOLL
SAVE's first report published in the *Architect's Journal*, 17 and 24 December 1975.

CONSERVATION AND JOBS
SAVE's second report published in *Built Environment Quarterly*, September 1976.

SAVE MENTMORE FOR THE NATION
A booklet about the treasures of Mentmore Towers, published in January 1977 as part of SAVE's campaign to preserve the house and contents for the nation. The collection was subsequently sold.

APPENDICES

OFF THE RAILS: SAVING RAILWAY ARCHITECTURE
The companion book to SAVE's first exhibition, which was held at the RIBA Heinz Gallery from January to March 1977.

LEFT TO ROT
A report highlighting the failure of the present legislation to prevent large numbers of listed buildings from falling into decay and giving recommendations on how the law could be improved. Published in the *Architect's Journal*, 22 November 1978.

PRESERVATION PAYS: Tourism & the Economic Benefits of Conserving Historic Buildings
Published in December 1978, providing detailed information on how conservation can bring both prosperity and jobs.

SATANIC MILLS: INDUSTRIAL ARCHITECTURE IN THE PENNINES
The companion book to SAVE's second exhibition at the RIBA Heinz Gallery, 31 January–11 April 1979, drawing attention to the architectural quality of the textile mills and the magic of the industrial landscape.

ELYSIAN GARDENS: A STRATEGY FOR THEIR SURVIVAL
Coincided with the V & A exhibition 'The Garden' in May 1979. It examined the need for protection for historic gardens, illustrating some famous gardens that have been lost and putting forward proposals for tackling the problems of maintaining great gardens.

DROWNING IN VAT
Before the 1984 Budget, VAT was charged on repairs but not on new work done to existing buildings, creating an incentive to alter rather than repair. Although VAT is now charged on alterations, there is still the anomaly of new construction remaining exempt. Published March 1980.

LOST HOUSES OF SCOTLAND
Since 1900, Scotland has lost at least 378 notable country houses. This book documented the losses and underlined the importance of the efforts being made to preserve, maintain and use those that remain. Published July 1980.

THE FALL OF ZION
Nonconformist chapels are closing at an increasing rate. This report is a major survey of Nonconformist architecture in the North. Published October 1980.

ONE DAMNED GEORGIAN BUILDING AFTER ANOTHER
Threats to three major groups of Georgian houses in central London: the Carburton Street triangle (now demolished), the Comyn Ching triangle (since refurbished) and a group of Georgian houses off Baker Street. Published April 1981.

SILENT MANSIONS: MORE COUNTRY HOUSES AT RISK
A second illustrated report on threatened houses. Published May 1981.

THE NEW ICONOCLASTS
This report took a critical look at the Church of England and its policy for dealing with redundant historic churches with reference to Anglican churches in the North of England. Published September 1981.

WEST MIDLANDS: HISTORIC BUILDINGS AT RISK
This report listed a large number of historic buildings in the West Midlands that were either standing empty, falling into disrepair or under threat. Published October 1981.

CITY CENTRE CARVE-UP
Alarmingly, in a number of large cities the 'clean sweep' approach is making a comeback in Leeds, Liverpool and Newcastle. Published May 1982.

TAKING THE PLUNGE: THE ARCHITECTURE OF BATHING
The companion book to SAVE's exhibition at the RIBA Heinz Gallery 26 May–10 July 1982. It draws attention to the variety and quality of swimming baths throughout Britain. Published May 1982.

THE COUNTRY HOUSE: TO BE OR NOT TO BE
An illustrated book providing detailed proposals for the rescue of problem country houses. Published August 1982.

SAVE GIBRALTAR'S HERITAGE
This report assessed the significance of Gibraltar's architectural heritage and urged for proper protection. Published October 1982.

SAVE ACTION GUIDE

VANISHING HOUSES OF ENGLAND
This report, sponsored by Jackson-Stops & Staff, illustrates some of the numerous country houses that have been demolished. Published January 1983.

ESTATE VILLAGES: WHO CARES?
A study of the fate of estate villages revealing just how rapidly their unique character is being eroded. Published February 1983.

PRESERVE AND PROSPER: THE WIDER ECONOMIC BENEFITS OF CONSERVING HISTORIC BUILDINGS
An assessment of places and areas where positive conservation policies have brought economic benefits. Published June 1983.

TIME GENTLEMEN PLEASE
Published September 1983 in association with CAMRA, this series of essays highlighted the remarkable range of pub architecture from remote country pubs to the jazz-age roadhouses of the 1920s and 1930s.

FROM SPLENDOUR TO BANALITY: REBUILDING THE CITY OF LONDON 1945–1983
A photographic survey of buildings demolished since the War, ranging from prestigious banking headquarters to warehouses and illustrating the modern buildings that have replaced them. Published November 1983.

MR LAWSON, YOU HAVE DAMNED OUR BEST HOPES FOR BRITAIN'S HISTORIC BUILDINGS
Lightning leaflet on the implications of the VAT changes proposed in the March 1984 budget. Proposals were modified as a result of numerous representations and for the first time some concessions were made for listed buildings.

THE AGONY OF GEORGIAN LIVERPOOL
Georgian buildings under threat, many owned by Liverpool City Council, which still seeks to demolish rather than rehabilitate them. Published August 1984.

CHATHAM HISTORIC DOCKYARD: ALIVE OR MOTHBALLED?
A report providing detailed proposals for the re-use of the remarkable historic buildings in Chatham Dockyard. Published October 1984.

SOUTH YORKS—BUILDINGS AT RISK
Catalogue of threatened historic buildings. Published November 1984.

LONDON'S CHURCHES ARE FALLING DOWN
Draws attention to a considerable number of churches under threat in the Diocese of London. Published April 1985.

ENDANGERED DOMAINS
More country houses at risk—the third SAVE publication highlighting houses in danger in England and Wales. Published August 1985.

LONDON AFTER LIVINGSTONE: AN AGENDA FOR ENGLISH HERITAGE
The abolition of the GLC heralds a new era for London's historic buildings and areas with English Heritage taking over the responsibilities of the former GLC Historic Buildings Division. Published April 1986.

LEEDS: A LOST OPPORTUNITY?
This report catalogues a wide variety of historic buildings in and around Leeds, at risk or threatened by new development. Published July 1986.

PAVILIONS IN PERIL
An illustrated report highlighting some fifty garden buildings: grottoes, temples, menageries, bathhouses, boathouses, teahouses, belvederes and gazebos which are currently at risk. Published July 1987.

CHURCHES: A QUESTION OF CONVERSION
An extensively illustrated (colour and b/w) book showing new uses for churches ranging from offices and housing to theatres and restaurants. Emphasis is on schemes respecting the character and integrity of churches. Published September 1987.

CONSERVATION—A CREDIT ACCOUNT
The spending on historic buildings in this country is meagre compared to the enormous economic benefits that accrue directly from preservation. Ways are suggested of encouraging conservation through tax allowances, wider grants and reduction of VAT. Published March 1988.

LET POULTRY LIVE AGAIN!
Published in June 1988 to coincide with the second public inquiry into redevelopment proposals for the No 1 Poultry site at the heart of the City of London.

APPENDICES

A FUTURE FOR FARM BUILDINGS
New uses for redundant but attractive historic farm buildings no longer used in modern farming, illustrated in b/w and colour. Guidelines for conversion are suggested together with information about grants available to make the most of these threatened buildings without spoiling their rural character. Published September 1988.

SAVE THE WOBURN CANOVA
Our lightning report highlighting the importance of Antonio Canova's statue of the Three Graces commissioned by the Duke of Bedford in 1815 and in danger, at that time, of exportation to America. Published February 1990.

BRIGHT FUTURE: THE RE-USE OF INDUSTRIAL BUILDINGS
This is the sequel to *The Country House: To Be or Not To Be* and *Churches: A Question of Conversion* and looks at practical ways of saving mills, warehouses, maltings, and other industrial buildings. Published April 1990.

HISTORIC HOSPITALS AT RISK
This is SAVE's second report on the plight of many listed hospital buildings owned by the Health Authority. To coincide with an NHS conference on 28 June 1990 it urges the sale and re-use of these valuable buildings.

NOBODY'S HOME: HISTORIC BUILDINGS IN SEARCH OF NEW OWNERS
The second catalogue of empty and decaying historic buildings that are in need of saving. This is the sequel to *Empty Quarters: The Listed Building of Your Dreams* and lists more than 150 buildings from all over the country including churches, mills, country houses and farm cottages. Published November 1990.

APPENDIX III
LIST OF ORGANIZATIONS

Grant-giving Bodies

English Heritage (the Historic Buildings & Monuments Commission), Fortress House, 23 Savile Row, London W1X 2BT, tel: 071 973 3000

The government's statutory advisor on historic buildings in England. Gives advice and grants towards repairs.

In Wales this is carried out by:
Cadw, Brunel House, 2 Fitzalan Road, Cardiff CF2 1UY, tel: 0222 465511

and in Scotland by:
Historic Buildings & Monuments Directorate Scottish Development Department, 20 Brandon Street, Edinburgh EH3 5RA, tel: 031 556 8400

National Heritage Memorial Fund, 10 St James's Street, London SW1A 1EF, tel: 071 930 0963
The largest source of public funds for preserving the most outstanding examples of the nation's heritage, including buildings, land and works of art.

Architectural Heritage Fund, 17 Carlton House Terrace, London SW1Y 5AW, tel: 071 925 0199
An independent charity providing low-interest, short-term loans for building preservation trusts and other charitable bodies undertaking the restoration of historic buildings.

Department of the Environment
Applications for spotlisting a building in England should be sent to:
Listing Branch, Department of the Environment, Lambeth Bridge House, Albert Embankment, London SE1 7SB

in Wales to:
DoE Welsh Office, Crown Building, Cathays Park, Cardiff CF1 3NQ

and in Scotland to:
DoE Scottish Office, 20 Brandon Street, Edinburgh EH3 5DX

Amenity Societies
The following societies must be notified by local authorities of listed building applications to demolish or alter buildings that fall within their remit:

Victorian Society, 1 Priory Gardens, Bedford Park, London W4 1TT, tel: 071 994 1019
Founded in 1958 to save the best examples of Victorian building and to promote interest in the art and architecture of the period.

Likewise for the Georgian period:
Georgian Group, 37 Spital Square, London E1 6DY, tel: 071 377 1722

157

SAVE ACTION GUIDE

For earlier, and vernacular buildings—particularly barns and wind and watermills: Society for the Protection of Ancient Buildings, 37 Spital Square London E1 6DY, tel: 071 377 1644

The Ancient Monuments Society, St Andrew by the Wardrobe, Queen Victoria Street, London EC4V 5DE, tel: 071 236 3934
Founded in 1924 for the study and conservation of ancient monuments, historic buildings of all ages and fine old craftsmanship.

Council for British Archaeology, 112 Kennington Road, London SE11 6RE, tel: 071 582 0494
Promotes the study and practice of archaeology throughout Britain. Comments on new road proposals.

Although not a statutory amenity society, the Thirties Society campaigns for better protection of twentieth-century architecture.
The Thirties Society, 58 Crescent Lane, London SW4 9PU, tel: 071 738 8480
The Civic Trust, 17 Carlton House Terrace, London SW1Y 5AW, tel: 071 930 0914
Provides support and advice for some 1,000 local amenity and civic societies. Promotes high standards of design, planning and restoration.

Churches
Historic Churches Preservation Trust, Fulham Palace, Bishop's Park, London SW6 6EA, tel: 071 736 3054
Has addresses of all local county churches trusts, and should be the first port of call for advice and information.

Redundant Churches Fund, St Andrew by the Wardrobe, Queen Victoria Street, London EC4V 5DE, tel: 071 248 7461
Funded partly by the Church of England and partly by the State, the Fund assumes responsibility for the maintenance and care of redundant Anglican churches of outstanding quality.

Council for the Care of Churches, 83 London Wall, London EC2M 5NA, tel: 071 638 0971
When closure of a church is suggested, the Council makes a detailed report and advises the Diocese on what should happen to the building.

Friends of Friendless Churches, St Andrew by the Wardrobe, Queen Victoria Street, London EC4V 5DE, tel: 071 248 7461
Without any state aid, the Friends take on churches that cannot be vested in the Redundant Churches Fund.

Other Building Types
The Cinemas & Theatres Association, 40 Winchester Street, London SW1V 4NF, tel: 071 834 0549

Historic Farm Buildings Group, c/o Centre of East Anglian Studies, University of East Anglia, Norwich NR4 7TJ, tel: 0603 592667
Specifically concerned with barns and other farm buildings of historic interest

The Landmark Trust, Shottesbrooke, Maidenhead, Berkshire, tel: 0628 823431
Acquires and restores unusual buildings of all types, which are then available for short-term lease.

Folly Fellowship, Woodstock House, Winterhill Way, Burpham, Surrey GU4 7JX
Formed to promote the study and protection of follies and other ornamental garden buildings

Countryside
The following organizations are concerned for the greater protection and preservation of the countryside in Great Britain:

Council for the Protection of Rural England, Warwick House, 25 Buckingham Palace Road, London SW1W 0PP, tel: 071 976 6433

Council for the Protection of Rural Wales, 31 High Street, Welshpool, Powys SY21 7JP, tel: 0938 552525

Association for the Protection of Rural Scotland, 14a Napier Road, Edinburgh EH10 5AY, tel: 031 229 1081

Nature Conservancy Council, Northminster House, Northminster Road, Peterborough PE1 1UA, tel: 0733 340345

Countryside Commission, John Dower House, Crescent Place, Cheltenham, Gloucestershire GL50 3RA, tel: 0242 521451

Rural Development Commission, 141 Castle Street, Salisbury SP1 3PP, tel: 0722 336255

INDEX

(Page numbers in italics refer to illustration captions)

A La Ronde, Exmouth, Devon, 36
All Saints Church, Sheffield, 79
All Souls Church, Halifax, 84–6
Architects Journal, 9, 11
Architectural Heritage Fund, 28
Article 4 Directions, 27
Arundel Castle, W Sussex, 37

Barlaston Hall, Staffs, 57–60
barns, 73–5
Battersea Power Station, 134–6
Baynards Park, Surrey, *35*
Belgrave Chapel, Darwen, Lancs, 12, *14*
Belton House, Lincs, 36, 37, 39
Bembridge Royal Spithead Hotel, Isle of Wight, *141*
Biddulph Grange, Staffs, 65–6
Billing Hall, Northants, *35*
Billingsgate Fish Market, 99, 118, 121–3
Bracken House, London, 102–3
Bright Future, 128, 130, 157
British Coal, *see* National Coal Board
British Rail, 137–8, 144
Brocklesby railway station, 12
Brodsworth Hall, S Yorks, 36, 37, 38, 44
Brynmawr Rubber Factory, Gwent, 132

Calke Abbey, Derbyshire, 36, 37, 38, 39
Callaly, Northd, 55
Callendar House, Falkirk, 56
campaigns, 20–30
Canterbury Cathedral, 102
Capel Manor stables, Enfield, 76
Carnwath, Robert, 59–60, 109
Carter Place Hall, Lancs, *35*
Cemetery Chapel, Amesbury, 79
'Change and Decay: the Future of our Churches' exhibition, 77
chapels, 93–6, 150–1
Chesterfield, 100, 118
churches, 14, 38, 77–98, 150–1; alternative uses, 91, 93–4; demolition, 78–9, 87–91; Nonconformist, 93–6, 150–1; redundant, 81–6; Scottish, 96–8; Welsh, 95–6
Churches: A Question of Conversion, 80, 156
Churches at Risk, 80
cinemas, 143–4
Concrete Jerusalem, The, 153
conservation: criteria, 18–19; garden, 65–8; reasons for, 7–8; role of architects, 8; value of, 99, 102

conservation areas, 18, 19, 26–8, 91, 110, 149–50, 151
Cookridge Street, No's 49–51, Leeds, *115*
Council for the Care of Churches, 81
country houses, 15–16, 33–60; demolished, 34–5, 48; empty, 45–53; in institutional use, 53–60; with contents, 33–45
Countryside Commission, 63, 74
Covent Garden, 118–19, 120–1
Crossley textile mill, Dean Clough, Halifax, 129
Cullen House, Banffshire, 55
Curtains!!! A New Life for Old Theatres, 143

Danson Hill, Bexleyheath, 56
'Destruction of the Country House' exhibition, 10, 33
Dingley, Northants, 55
Duddingston, Edinburgh, 50

East Street Methodist Chapel, Tonbridge, Kent, 95
Empty Quarters, 12, 14, 47
Endangered Domains, 12, 50, 156
English Heritage, 11, 26, 37, 60, 62, 63, 74, 86, 88, 93, 109, 149, 151, 152
Environment, Department of, 25, 26, 27, 42, 52–3, 60, 84, 94, 100, 103, 106, 107, 150, 151, 154

facades, 110–12
Fall of Zion, The, 93, 155
Farrell, Terry, 17, 104
Fitzwilliam Amenity Trust, 71
follies, 69, 71
Frogmore House, Windsor, 38
Future for Farm Buildings, A, 73, 157

garden conservation, 65–8, 151–2
Garden History Society, 64, 152
Gate Burton, Lincs, *70*
George Inn, Nailsworth, Glos, *142*
George Inn, Southwark, *140*
Gilcomston Church, Aberdeen, 97, 98
grading, 154
Grange, The, Hants, 52–3
Grovelands, 56
Guildhall School of Music, 111
Gunton, Norfolk, 55, 63

Hackfall, N Yorks, 66–7, *68*
Halifax, 153
Halswell House, Somerset, 71
Hampton Court House, 71–2

Hartwell House, Bucks, 54–5
Hazells, The, Beds, 55
Henham Hall, Suffolk, *35*
Herstmonceux Castle, E Sussex, 50–1
Heseltine, Michael, 20, 59, 121, 123, 135, 146, 148
Highclere Park, Hants, 64
Highcliffe Castle, Dorset, 56
historic buildings: abandoned, 12–14; conversion, 19; councils, 69, 149; grading, 154; grants, 153; maintenance, 28–9; preservation trusts, 28; refurbishment, 106–7; spotlisting, 25–6
Historic Buildings and Monuments Commission for England, *see* English Heritage
Historic Buildings Council, 59, 69, 84, 102, 149, 154
Historic Buildings Council for Scotland, 97, 98
Historic Churches Preservation Trust, 81, 82
Hollein, Hans, 114
Holy Name, Church of the, Manchester, 92
Holy Trinity, Church of the, Birkenhead, 79
Holy Trinity, Church of the, Burnley, 14
Holy Trinity, Church of the, Rugby, 78
Holme Lacey, Herefordshire, 44
Hospitals: A Suitable Case for Treatment, 126
hotels, 141–2
Hylands, nr Chelmsford, 56

Ice House Hunt, 71

Jack Straw's Castle, Hampstead, 11, *13*
Jenkins, Simon, 11, 22, 23, 137
Jubilee Hall, Covent Garden, 120–1

Kedleston Hall, Derbyshire, 36, 37, 38

Lamb and Lion Yard, Farnham, *101*
Landmark Trust, 67, 69, *70*
landscape parks, 62–4
Langley Station, Slough, Berks, *139*
Leeds Castle, Kent, 37
Leeds Market, *119*
legal action, 29–30
Lifford Hall, Birmingham, *48*
listed buildings, 12, 18, 19, 20–1, 25–6, 28, 107, 148–9, 154

159

SAVE ACTION GUIDE

Llangoed Hall, Powys, 47
local authority, *see* planning authority
Lost Houses of Scotland, 48, 155
Lost Houses of Wales, 46–7
Lowell, Massachusetts, 131, 153
Lyceum, the, Liverpool, 144–6

Manchester, 119
Manifold Trust, 59
Mansion House Square, London, 104–5
Mappin and Webb, 16, 17, 104
Martin, Kit, 55–6, 58
Mavisbank, nr Edinburgh, 52
media, use of, 22–5
mental hospitals, 125–6
Mentmore Towers, Bucks, 36, 38, 39–43
Merrow Grange, Surrey, 68
Methodist Chapel, Sproxton, Lincs, 11, 12
Middlethorpe Hall, York, 55
mills, 128–32
Moat House, Fisher's Pond, Hants, 75
Monkton House, W Sussex, 36
Moot, The, Downton, 66

National Coal Board, 43–5, 59, 60
National Heritage Act (1983), 151
National Heritage Memorial Fund, 37, 42, 43, 60, 66, 85, 86
National Land Fund, 42
National Parks Authority, 74
National Trust, 36, 37, 38, 42, 43, 66
New End Hospital, Hampstead, 125, 126–7
Nobody's Home, 48, 157
Nutfield Priory, Reigate, 57

Oak Hill Mansion, Accrington, 56
'Off the Rails' exhibition, 137

Paca House, Annapolis, 68
parks, 147, 151–2
Pavilion Theatre, Ryde, 11
Pavilions in Peril, 69, 156
Paxton Park, Cambs, 34
Pell Wall Hall, Market Drayton, Shropshire, 52, 53, 54
petitions, 21–2
Pevsner, Sir Nikolaus, 145, 148

photographs, 24, 26
pillar boxes, 116
Pitt Street Baths, Portsmouth, 105
planning authority, 13, 25, 26, 27, 28–9, 152
planning permission, 20, 50–1, 55
Plas Teg, Clwyd, 47
Pontysgaryd, Powys, 46
Poultry, No 1, London, 99, 104, 150
Preservation Pays, 102, 155
press releases, 23–4
pubs, 140–1

railways, 117
Railway Heritage Trust, 137–8, 139
Redundant Churches Fund, 82, 83, 84, 150
Register of Historic Parks and Gardens, 151–2
Repairs Notices, 28–9, 152–3
Repton, Humphry, 61, 62, 64
road proposals, 62, 64
Robinwood Mill, Todmorden, Lancs, 132
Rodboro Buildings, Guildford, 133
Roehampton Estate, 149
Rogers, Richard, 121, 122
Rose Theatre, Southwark, 143
Royal Infirmary, Sheffield, 125
Royal Infirmary, Shrewsbury, 125
Royal Victoria Patriotic Building, Wandsworth, 125

St Francis Xavier, Church of, Liverpool, 89–91
St George's Hospital, London, 112
St John the Baptist, Church of, Avon Dassett, Warwickshire, 82–4, 87
St Mark's Church, North Audley Street, London, 80–1
St Mary-in-the-Castle, Church of, Hastings, 87–8
St Stephen's Church, Newcastle upon Tyne, 79
Salt's Mill, Saltaire, Bradford, 129, 130
Sandys, Duncan, 26, 150
'Satanic Mills' exhibition, 130–1
Save the Woburn Canova, 109, 157
Scotland, 48–9, 96–8, 150
Scotland's Endangered Houses, 49

Scourge of Britain's High Streets, The, 113
seaside towns, 153
shopping developments, 99–101
Silent Mansions, 12, 45, 50, 155
Smardale Gill, Cumbria, 138
Spitalfields Market, London, 99, 118
Spixworth Hall, Norfolk, 34
Stout's Hill, nr Stroud, 55
street architecture, 16, 110
summer houses, 150
Sustrans Trust, 138

temples, 71
Theatres Trust, 143
Thoresby Hall, Notts, 36, 38, 43–5
Three Graces, the, Woburn Abbey, 107–9
Tithe Barn, Pilton, Somerset, 75
Tomorrow's Ruins, 12, 50
tourism, 8, 102
Tranby Lodge, Humberside, 35
trusts, 28, 37, 67
Tynighame, E Lothian, 55

Uffington Park, Lincs, 12, 63
Unitarian Chapel, Northgate, Halifax, 79
United Reformed Church, Headingley Hill, Leeds, 94

Vanishing Houses of England, 50, 156
Victoria and Albert Museum, 10, 15, 33, 77, 109
Victorian Society, 148

Wales, 46–7, 95–6, 150
warehouses, 128–9
Weeks, Stephen, 95, 138
Welbeck Abbey, 43
Wentworth Castle, 53
Wentworth Woodhouse, Yorks, 53, 71
West Hill Hospital, Dartford, Kent, 126
White Paper on the Environment, 130
Woodland Trust, 66

Yerbeston Church, Dyfed, 96
Ynysymaengwyn, Gwynedd, 46